A DARK HISTORY
PHILOSOPHY

STUDIES IN CONTINENTAL THOUGHT

John Sallis, *editor*

Consulting Editors

Robert Bernasconi
John D. Caputo
David Carr
Edward S. Casey
David Farrell Krell
Lenore Langsdorf

James Risser
Dennis J. Schmidt
Calvin O. Schrag
Charles E. Scott
Daniela Vallega-Neu
David Wood

A DARK HISTORY OF MODERN PHILOSOPHY

Bernard Freydberg

Indiana University Press

This book is a publication of

Indiana University Press
Office of Scholarly Publishing
Herman B Wells Library 350
1320 East 10th Street
Bloomington, Indiana 47405 USA

iupress.indiana.edu

© 2017 by Bernard Freydberg

All rights reserved

No part of this book may be reproduced or utilized in any form or by any means, electronic or mechanical, including photocopying and recording, or by any information storage and retrieval system, without permission in writing from the publisher. The Association of American University Presses' Resolution on Permissions constitutes the only exception to this prohibition.

♾ The paper used in this publication meets the minimum requirements of the American National Standard for Information Sciences—Permanence of Paper for Printed Library Materials, ANSI Z39.48-1992.

Manufactured in the United States of America

Cataloging information is available from the Library of Congress.

ISBN 978-0-253-02935-5 (cloth)
ISBN 978-0-253-02946-1 (paperback)
ISBN 978-0-253-03024-5 (ebook)

1 2 3 4 5   22 21 20 19 18 17

To Akiko Kotani
"I would not wish any companion
in the world but you."
—*The Tempest,* act 3, scene 1

Contents

Acknowledgments ix

Preliminary Matters 1

1 Fissures in the History of Modern Philosophy 11

Prelude: On Anteriority 33

2 Spinoza's Abysmal Rationalism 39

Intermezzo: On the Putative History of German Idealism 81

3 Unruly Greek Schelling 87

Coda: Nietzsche as Crux 123

Bibliography 131
Index 137

Acknowledgments

This, my most ambitious book to date, took a very long time to complete. From the outset, I believed strongly that the guiding idea was both original and worthwhile. At the onset of my work on it, I was grievously overconfident both as an author and as a thinker. Somehow I supposed that if I "loosened up" and wrote from "inspired intuition," the impact would be stunning. Fueled by this conceit, I completed a draft several years ago. The two close friends to whom I sent it, Richard Findler and Christopher Yates, each responded that they supported the idea, but ever so gently let me know that the writing did not communicate well at all.

I am very grateful for their valuable input, which saved me from the embarrassment I would surely have suffered had I submitted it for potential (and hopeless) publication. I knew at once that the draft was a disaster. I attempted two all-out revisions, and concluded firmly that I did not have to trouble these two fine philosophers again. My own reading confirmed its disheartening incomprehensibility. It sat on the shelf, and when I was asked what my next large project would be, I told them that I had a pretty good idea for my would-be ninth book but was too stupid to write it.

At the 2015 Society for Phenomenology and Existential Philosophy meeting in Atlanta, the last paper I heard before I had to head to the airport was on the role of reason in Schelling, presented by Mark Thomas. I had not known of the presenter earlier. but the penetrating discernment of his paper thrilled me and provoked me. The Q and A that took place between Mark Thomas, my dear friend Dennis J. Schmidt, who moderated, and me somehow dislodged the boulder in my head. I had a guiding thread for *A Dark History of Modern Philosophy*: Anteriority. I took the early failed drafts off the shelf, and with surprising alacrity managed to complete it in just a few months. Big thanks also go to Mark Thomas and Denny Schmidt.

Once again, I am very grateful to Michael Rudar for both his work on the text and his helpful critical comments. Kathleen Manning remains the great librarian that she always has been, and her friendship is as valuable as her excellent work.

Above all, the ongoing dialogue with my brilliant, encouraging, and beloved wife Akiko Kotani continues to inspire me beyond measure. Once again, my dedication in all things, this book included, is to her.

A DARK HISTORY OF MODERN PHILOSOPHY

Preliminary Matters

The history of modern philosophy is usually and, in some sense appropriately, presented in courses as a progression through its major figures. Most such courses begin with Descartes, proceed by chronologically grouping the "rationalists" and the "empiricists," and complete this survey with Kant, who is seen as attempting to unify both strains. Both strains, taken separately or together, appraised the role of reason. All the major thinkers of this period took for granted that the determination of reason's role is a central theme in modern philosophy. My purpose here does not involve disputing something so obvious. However, this very obviousness has long provoked an uneasy discomposure in me that I could not properly locate until now.

Though I believe that this discovery answers many of the questions that troubled me, the discomposure nevertheless remains. It remains because such unease belongs inherently to the history of modern philosophy. By this, I mean that the great era of modern philosophy took its departure from another great era, that of Greek thought. But in so doing, modern philosophy suppressed that dark, Delphic region accessible by nonrational means alone. Suppression, however, does not and cannot mean elimination, cancellation, and can never mean *Aufhebung*, Hegel's term that includes negating, overcoming and surpassing. The dark origin of modern philosophy roils everywhere beneath its rational surface, giving modern philosophy life even as its progeny seek to deny this darkness. *A Dark History of Modern Philosophy* seeks to expose this crucially concealed dimension.

The heart of this discourse consists in the excavation of those dark sources as they exercise their potency, which is mostly unacknowledged and always silent concerning their significance. The first large chapter presents a survey of the major figures in the history of modern philosophy, with the exception of Spinoza. Spinoza merits special consideration, which his thought will receive at the proper time. This survey differs markedly from more accustomed ones in that it concentrates on the unavoidable limits that stop thought in its tracks. This is as far as possible from an attempt at refutation. Rather, such limits belong to the very nature of philosophy itself. "Indeed, it is precisely in knowing its limits that philosophy consists."[1] The thinkers of this period earned their renown through the new vistas opened by their work, but also—and of at least equal significance, in my view—by the regions that their insights could not enter in principle.

Even with this in mind, however, a prejudice may lead to the customary view that philosophy is doctrinal above all. Students on all levels who are examined on, for example, Leibniz and Hume, provide "correct" answers, stating that the former is a rationalist who believes in a preestablished harmony, and the latter is an empiricist who believes that the causal principle is rationally unfounded. In this book, I attempt to turn attention away from the doctrines and toward those realms rendered inaccessible by modern means. In other words, at the juncture where thought breaks off, the most intriguing areas of all solicit our apprehension. I call these junctures *fissures*.[2] Here, I reverse the order dictated by the customary prejudice. That is, rather than hold that the boundary that limits the doctrine gives rise to the fissures, I maintain that the fissures make the doctrines possible at all—that is, the fissures animate the doctrines.

Accordingly, the task of the first chapter concerns an examination of each of the major modern thinkers, and it aims to expose the gap—the fissure or fissures—that provides ballast to the positive analyses offered in their texts. The fissures take absolutely nothing away from the unquestioned power, and/or validity, and/or value of their work. On the contrary, the fissures vouchsafe the worth of the works in a way that no sophisticated attempt to paper them over ever could.

How, then, can we find a path to those regions that, although long concealed from view, give rise to epoch-making thought concerning the role of reason that would deny them acknowledgment? The entryway extends through ancient Greek poetry, and in ancient Greek philosophy that is interpreted in a particular way. The significance of both Greek poetry and its role in Greek philosophy come together in Plato's *Ion*. This long passage also gives the lie decisively to the often-held "truism" that Plato treated poetry with hostility and sought to ban it from his so-called and wrongly called Ideal City.[3]

> Socrates: ... [a]s I said earlier, speaking well about Homer is not something that you have mastered, but a divine power that moves you, as a stone that moves iron rings. Euripides calls it a Magnet, but to

the many it is known as Heraclean. This stone not only pulls iron rings, but also imparts to them a similar power of pulling other rings, and sometimes you may see a number of pieces of iron and rings suspended from one another so as to form quite a long chain. And the power in all of them derives their power of suspension from the original stone. In like manner the Muse herself first of all inspires people; and from these inspired persons a chain of other persons is suspended, who receive the inspiration (*enthousiasmos*). For all good poets, epic as well as lyric, compose their beautiful poems not by art, but because they are inspired and possessed. And as the Corybantian revelers when they dance are not in their right mind, so the lyric poets are not in their right mind when they are composing their beautiful strains: but when falling under the power of music and meter they are inspired and possessed, like Bacchic maidens who draw milk and honey from the rivers when they are under the influence of Dionysus but not when they are in their right mind.... And this is true. For the poet is a light and winged and holy thing, and there is no invention in him until he has been inspired and is out of his senses, and the mind is no longer in him: when he has not attained to this state, he is powerless and is unable to utter his oracles....

God takes away the mind (*nous*) of poets, and uses them as his servants, as he also uses diviners and holy prophets, in order that we who hear them may know them to be speaking not of themselves who utter these priceless words in a state of unconsciousness, but that God himself is the speaker, and that through them he is conversing with us.... For in this way, the God would seem to indicate to us and not allow us to doubt that these beautiful poems are not human, or the work of human beings, but divine and the work of God; and that the poets are only the interpreters of the Gods by whom they are severally possessed. Was not this the lesson which the God intended to teach when by the mouth of the worst of poets he sang the best of songs? Am I not right, Ion?

The spectator constitutes the final link in the chain first inspired by the god, and the spectator enters the chain by inspiration as well. The contemporary reader should not be misled into interpreting *enthousiasmos* as "enthusiasm" in its common understanding. As Plato's *Phaedrus* reports, *enthousiasmos* in the Muses constitutes the third form of divine madness. Divine madness differs markedly from human madness in that unlike the harmful unruliness begotten by human madness, divine madness always involves the introduction of measure.[4]

How can inspiration take place (1) in modern terms? How can it take place (2) in contemporary terms? A response to (1) can be unearthed from Kant's *Critique of Judgment*, in which the role of understanding is diminished. Imagination, which plays a principal role in the first critique and, in my view, in the second as well,[5] is enhanced in the third. The judgment of beauty consists in the agreement of imagination and understanding resulting from their free play; no concept can be involved in this reflective judgment. The judgment of sublimity consists in the notion of magnitude of an object that is too large for the imagination but does not reach the infinitude of reason.[6] This disharmony provokes a consciousness of one's moral vocation, which stands outside the ream of all sensation.

Kant's markedly prosaic analogue to Platonic inspiration occurs in his notion of genius, a notion prepared by the detaching of concepts from the two kinds of reflective judgments concerning beauty and sublimity. Of beautiful art, he writes: "*Genius* is the talent (or natural gift) that gives the rule to Art. Since talent, as the innate productive faculty of the artist, belongs itself to Nature, we may express the matter thus: *Genius* is the innate mental disposition (*ingenium*) through which Nature gives the rule to Art. (#46)." Genius, which cannot be taught, is the necessary but not sufficient condition for beautiful art; taste is required as well. Though this seems to travel far from divine madness, its nonconceptual formulation establishes a kinship (at least of sorts) between them.

The answer to (2), concerning inspiration in a contemporary sense, will occur first in the chapter on the hyperrational Spinoza, next in the central chapter on Schelling, and finally, most definitively, in the brief Coda on Nietzsche. In my own effort to fathom the nether substrata beneath the various surfaces, I shall draw upon that Platonic trust (*pistis*), even in mythos and especially in the great myth that makes itself manifest at several places in the *Phaedrus*,[7] and shall place reason offstage in favor of a mix of learning and divination. Spinoza presented the obvious difficulty that the only Greek who influenced his writing is Euclid, who merely provided the external form of Spinoza's *Ethics*. However, his insistence on the oneness of an imminent, impersonal God did inspire those thinkers of German Idealism for whom such oneness had an essential place, as we will soon see.

Schelling furnishes the most ample stimulus for thought among the moderns—if indeed he can properly be numbered among them. He certainly descends from Kant and especially from Fichte; his first several books take their departure expressly from the Fichtean problematic. In

Schelling's most notable and final published work, *Freiheitsschrift*,[8] one can discern many echoes from Kant's *Religion within the Limits of Reason Alone*. However, unlike his two forebears and contemporaries, he claimed that like art, philosophy had its own peculiar raptures, its own inspirations. Though at times he seemed to agree with his contemporary Hegel that Christianity is the apotheosis of religion and of humanity, the content of much of his work militates against this view. Two other antecedents complicate the picture, one much more recent than the other.

The more recent one is the aforementioned Spinoza, whose equation of God with nature in the *Ethics* certainly outraged those who had belief (or at least a stake) in a supernatural God, but the more trenchant views that were published posthumously in *Theological-Political Treatise* raised the affront by several orders of magnitude. The threads that connect this work consist of contempt for the superstition according to which the vast majority of humans practice whatever religion they hold, and an accompanying contempt for that same majority who are incapable of governing themselves by the "simple" rules of reason.[9]

Although Kant displayed only very limited interest in Spinoza (and limited understanding of his thought as well), Fichte found much that was worthy there. Fichte took pains to fashion a Kantian Doctrine of Science (*Wissenschaftslehre*), deriving it from a single governing principle. Like Schelling, Hölderlin, and Hegel during their student years together, he took to heart the ancient motto *hen kai pan* (one is all), from the Presocratics. And Schelling's modern paradigm, guided by this motto, was Spinozism (as was the case of the other aforementioned thinkers, although they had somewhat different slants). This is because Spinoza presented a system of the whole derived from a single source, and therefore presented a fully developed and complete architecture from which his departure could begin.

While Fichte critiqued Spinoza for presenting a system in which his fundamental principle, the I (*das Ich*), could not appear, for Schelling its absence of life indicated what was lacking in it. This lack could only be made good by love (eros), which would animate the system and transform it from its dry and dogmatic form into a living, human system of freedom that would embrace evil as one of its necessary constituents. In order to arrive at this system, Schelling had to go on a voyage that Fichte could not, into the dark depths where Christianity cannot reach. The language of reason and argument had to admit another language as the way downward, the language of Greek myth. On the descent, the figures and events to which Greek myth gave birth also had to be granted entry. The dialogues of Plato stand on the cusp, bridging rational language and mythical language. Logos could still signify mythos, and often did.[10] The *Timaeus* served as a principal touchstone for Schelling from the earliest phases of his career, as seen in his special attention to that most obscure of notions, the *chora*. The recent revival of Schelling and Schelling interpretation in Continental thought takes place beside and in association with the revival in Plato interpretation heralded by John Sallis's *Being and Logos: Reading the Platonic Dialogues*. In the latter, mythos, the mythical content, is raised to an equal status with logos, the content disclosed through arguments. Logos and mythos are the first two elements. The third element, *ergon* (deed) concerns the interactions of the interlocutors and the various jests, gestures, and asides that occur throughout.[11]

Schelling's discourse began in a form that melded the philosophical prose of Kant and Fichte with the Spinozist deductive form. Propositions are presented in bold type, followed generally by discussions and descriptions of varying length and detail.[12] However, this form proved to be unable to contain many of his pivotal insights, which exceeded the boundaries he had set. As in many if not all great thinkers, this did not constitute a weakness or flaw, but rather an overabundance that gives birth to fresh questioning.

This excess for the most part concerned image and imagination. In Plato's *Republic*, no sooner were images relegated to the lowest rung of the divided line at the end of Book VI than they were called upon for heavy lifting in the first words of Book VII: "Next, then, make an image" (514a). This was followed by a superabundance of concern with images, culminating in its finale, the myth of Er, which takes place entirely below the earth in Hades. Kant's blind, dark, productive imagination is the source of all synthesis.[13] Thus, the Pure Concepts of the Understanding—Reason's most salient contribution to any knowledge claims—prove to be insufficient for *any* knowledge, but require Schemata that originate from (once again) the dark depths of the human soul—that is, from unreason. Schelling's thought belongs to this noble lineage of self-generated excess.

Schelling's notion of imagination is considerably more expansive than Plato's or Kant's. The divine imagination becomes primary in his thought. This constitutes a remarkable difference from the more traditional modern philosophers whose doctrines either relegated imagination to a lower status due to its capricious nature. It also differs radically from Spinoza, who discredited it categorically at times. Did Schelling suppose that he knew more than these others? He certainly did not. Instead, as I attempted to demonstrate in my earlier Schelling book,[14] Schelling's unprecedented language incorporated mythos with its poetically creative sensibility into the discourse of Kant and Fichte. A similar sensibility must enter Schelling's texts in order to harvest their philosophical bounties.

In Spinoza, the suppression of the dark and living region of philosophy's history is so thoroughgoing that access to it requires the closest attention in order to discover the entryways to this obscure region. By contrast, in Schelling the dark region becomes explicit and moves to prominence alongside the brighter manifestation of reason and rule. In the Coda on Nietzsche, mythos takes over. The Apollinian/Dionysian duplicity (*Duplizität*) not only replaces reason as the basis of philosophy but also demotes it to a weak, second-order recourse when the age cannot sustain the health and vitality demanded by the two artistic gods. In this way, the genuine history of modern philosophy that I propose here countermands the view that the refinement of reason's role constitutes the result of philosophy's history, and implicitly suggests that philosophy since Nietzsche must take place not in light of any new discoveries, but in acknowledging the darkness that always dwells beneath.

The path of the book moves through the main phases discussed above, but with two additional short sections connecting them. Chapter 1, "Fissures in the History of Modern Philosophy," follows this introduction. "Prelude: On Anteriority" imparts the guiding thread that ties together all that follows, and the role it plays in mining the shadowy realm beneath. Chapter 2 ensues, titled "Spinoza's Abysmal Rationalism."

Before the vital Schelling chapter, I present an "Intermezzo: On the Putative History of German Idealism," in which I attempt to demonstrate another virtually unprecedented view, namely, of Hegel as a positive precursor to the philosophy of Schelling, his contemporary. Chapter 3, "Unruly Greek Schelling" follows. The book concludes with a Coda on Nietzsche that draws especially on his "Attempt at a Self-Criticism." This Coda carries through the previously concealed history to its most manifest disclosure.

As an almost inviolable rule, I avoid neologisms. They are all too often pretentious and useless. However, I beg the reader's pardon, and ask for both indulgence and even for forgiveness: in this book, I provide *endarkenment*.

Notes

1. Immanuel Kant, *Critique of Pure Reason*, trans. Norman Kemp Smith (New York: St. Martin's Press, 1965), A727, B755.
2. See John Sallis, *Being and Logos: Reading the Platonic Dialogues* (Bloomington: Indiana University Press, 1996); and Bernard Freydberg, *The Play of the Platonic Dialogues* (New York: Peter Lang, 1997).
3. See Sallis, *Being and Logos*; and Freydberg, *Play of the Platonic Dialogues*.
4. See Plato's *Phaedrus*, 244a–245c. The four types of divine madness are: (1) prophesy guided by inspiration, which reins in excess; (2) healing of ancient maladies and curses; (3) inspiration by the Muses, who inspire humans to create poetry in melody and meter; and (4) *eros*, the kind of love placed only in service to the beloved.
5. In Bernard Freydberg, *Imagination in Kant's Critique of Practical Reason* (Bloomington: University of Indiana Press, 2005), I present the case that Kant's attempt to avoid imagination in his practical (moral) philosophy cannot be successful on any level. Imagination is the source of all synthesis. The indispensable principles of moral philosophy, for example, the categorical imperative and its iterations, are one and all synthetic a priori.
6. See Immanuel Kant, *Critique of Judgment*, trans. J. H. Bernard (Indianapolis: Hafner, 1964). Kant divides this into the mathematical sublime and the dynamical sublime. "Sublime" refers to what is absolutely great as apprehended by the mind that judges. The mathematically sublime consists of the apprehension of something by comparison with which everything else is small, or in other words, the mathematically sublime mind has the ability to think in a way that surpasses every standard of sense (#25). The dynamically sublime refers to the mind's judgment of absolute *might*, which produces the temporary disharmony of the faculties such that fear and pain are experienced. Once the fear passes, joy occurs and the mind becomes aware of its own power and its disposition toward the infinite as its rational destiny (#26). (Note: #25 and #26 are the section numbers as they occur in the text.)
7. At *Phaedrus* 229c–230b, Socrates rejects the view of the "wise ones" (*sophizmenoi*), who would explain away the myth of Boreas and Oreithyia by attributing her sudden egress from the mountain to natural causes, such as a strong wind. Affirming the common view, that is, truth of the myth, Socrates uses it as a springboard to question its importance for him in the pursuit of self-knowledge. The central image of the *Phaedrus*, is the great myth of *Eros* (244e–257a). Socrates calls the myth that begins with the praises of divine madness a *proof* (*apodeixis*). The modern and contemporary sense of *apodeixis* (apodeictic) indicates an indisputable insight or

conclusion. This is not the case for Plato. The root word in Greek is *apo-deiknumai*, "to show from." Thus a myth may have as much or more purchase on *apodeixis* than a "rational account." These same "wise ones" are chided in the following striking passage concerning the myth: "the proof shall be one which the wise will receive, and the merely clever disbelieve" (245c).

8. Its full title is *Philosophische Untersuchungen über das Wesen der menschlichen Freiheit und die damit zusammenhängenden Gegenstände*.

9. When one reads the posthumously published *A Theological-Political Treatise*, one ceases to wonder at the anger and enmity he provoked. His views were also quite well-known during his lifetime:

> I inquired why the Hebrews were called God's chosen people, and discovering that it was only because God had chosen for them a certain strip of territory, where they might live peaceably and at ease, I learnt that the Law revealed by God to Moses was merely the law of the individual Hebrew state, therefore that it was binding on none but Hebrews, and not even on Hebrews after the downfall of their nation. (Spinoza, *A Theological-Political Treatise*, ed. Jonathan Israel [Cambridge: Cambridge University Press, 2007], 9)

> I have often wondered, that persons who make a boast of professing the Christian religion, namely, love, joy, peace, temperance, and charity to all men, should quarrel with such rancorous animosity, and display daily towards one another such bitter hatred, that this, rather than the virtues they claim, is the readiest criterion of their faith. (Ibid., 7)

There are many ironies concerning Spinoza, the most gentle and moral of human beings in response to the venom he received, and his quiet insistence on the freedom of thought even in the face of his denial of free will or contingency in the events of the world.

10. Again, see Sallis, *Being and Logos*, 1–22.

11. Ibid.

12. See two examples among many: *Neue Deduktion des Naturrechts* (1796) and *Darstellung meines Systems der Philosophie* (1801), both in Schelling, *Sämmtliche Werke*, ed. K. F. A. Schelling (Stuttgart & Augsburg: J. G. Cotta, 1860).

13. "Synthesis in general, as we shall hereafter see, is the mere result of the power of imagination, a blind but indispensable function of the soul, without which we should have no knowledge whatsoever, but of which we are scarcely ever conscious. To bring this synthesis to concepts is a function which belongs to the understanding, and it is through this function of the understanding that we first obtain knowledge properly so called" (Kant, *Critique of Pure Reason*, A78, B103).

14. Bernard Freydberg, *Schelling's Dialogical Freedom Essay: Provocative Philosophy Then and Now* (Albany: State University of New York Press, 2008).

1 Fissures in the History of Modern Philosophy

Despite the customary practice of treating the history of modern philosophy as the evolution of fundamentally coherent doctrine, heterogeneity is an unmistakable feature in the thought of Descartes, Leibniz, Locke, Berkeley, and Kant. *Hetero-geneity*, "other-birthing" or "other-genus" summons thought to the fissure, the gap that allows for its occurrence. This characteristic can take surprising shapes and can lead to unexpected developments. Spinoza as the most rigorous of the rationalists and Hume as the most rigorous of the empiricists leave little or no room for a gap between different sources that bear upon our condition. However, even in these thinkers one can discern abysses, fissures that open onto dark regions where sight becomes most difficult, and another way of sensing is required.

What I am proposing is the following alteration of the standard narrative even as it seems most incontestable. The divisions within the standard narrative do not concern—at least do not essentially concern—the role of "reason" on one side and the role of "experience" on the other. Rather, both of these putative divisions respond to the darkness to which we are all given over. While this darkness can be called by many names, it escapes all of them: abyss, ignorance, death, impenetrability, Hades. At *Theaetetus* 155c, the eponymous figure around whom the dialogue takes place, confesses that he finds himself wondering excessively (*hyperphyos*), to which Socrates famously replies that all philosophy begins in wonder and that wonder is the mark of the philosopher.

The nature of the concealment I shall attempt to disclose finds its precursor in Aristotle's response to the matter of wonder. While wonder is the origin of all philosophy, its overcoming in *epistêmê*—in knowledge or in "science"—constitutes its purpose or end, its telos. Aristotle's creation of a series of sciences, from physics through psychology and animal studies to meteorology—not to mention metaphysics, logic, and aesthetics, which remain proper philosophical disciplines—bears out his "post-wonder" ambitions. Since Aristotle was wrong on a vast majority of even his most fundamental scientific pronouncements according to more recent and contemporary developments, there can be no doubt that seventeenth- and eighteenth-century developments in physics and mathematics inspired the great philosophers of this period; it has even been claimed that, despite the qualitative advances by Newton, Leibniz, and others, it was still possible for one person to "know everything there is to know" in the natural sciences and mathematics.

Descartes

When both sides of the current philosophical divide agree on a particular matter, my rule of thumb is to regard both sides as mistaken and to proceed under that assumption until proven wrong. In the case of René Descartes, this rule of thumb has provided the correct course. In the thought of Descartes, long honored with what I consider faint praise as the more-or-less bumbling but important founder of modern philosophy, both Anglo-American and Continental philosophers find a doctrine called "mind–body dualism." They are led to this view by passages such as the following:

> Now my first observation here is that there is a great difference between a mind and a body in that a body, by its very nature, is always divisible. On the other hand, a mind is always indivisible. For when I consider my mind, that is, myself insofar as I am only a thinking thing, I cannot distinguish any parts within me; I understand myself to be manifestly one complete thing. Although the entire mind seems to be united to the entire body, nevertheless, were a foot or an arm or any other bodily part to be amputated, I know that nothing has been taken away from the mind on that account. Nor can the faculties of willing, sensing, and understanding, and so on be called "parts" of the mind, since it is one and the same mind that wills, senses, and understands. On the other hand there is no corporeal or extended thing I can think of that in my thought easily divides into parts; and in this way I understand that it is divisible. This consideration alone would suffice to teach me that the soul is wholly diverse from the body, had I not yet known it well enough in any other way.[1]

Descartes's declaration of a "vast" difference between mind and body clearly refers to a quantitative difference, or more precisely to a difference that remains within the realm of mathematics: "divisibility" and "indivisibility" are mathematical concepts. By employing the well-known Latin distinction between thinking substance (*res cogitans*) and extended substance (*res extensa*), this vast difference between mind and body amounts to a difference for and within *res cogitans*. Bodies so conceived are nothing more and nothing less than the objects of pure geometry.

But what about those entities that are normally considered to be bodies? What about (to list several items from Descartes's text) hands, head, feet, sky, earth, and sea? What about feelings of hunger and thirst, and of pleasure and pain? What is their status? At first, Descartes ascribes our knowledge of them to "nature"; but upon attaining more self-knowledge he sees these very differently, though hardly less paradoxically: "For clearly these sensations of hunger, thirst, and so on, etc., are nothing but confused modes of thinking, arising from the union and, as it were, intermingling of the mind with the body."[2]

Hunger and thirst, pleasure and pain as confused thoughts—what can this mean? Can it mean, for example, that a toothache that requires root canal surgery is a confused thought in the way, perhaps, that the attempt to grasp the proof of an abstruse theorem in higher mathematics results in confused thought? I strongly suggest that the answer is affirmative. In the *Discourse on Method*, Descartes called the human body "a machine made by God," a phrase that offends many of my contemporary Continental colleagues who ascribe more differentiated qualities to bodies, often at the expense of the analogous qualities once located in souls. What he meant, and what has by and large determined the course of most successful Western medicine since, is that like all bodies the human body behaves in accord with mechanical laws.

For Descartes, such laws were regular unchanging fixed laws, as distinguished from teleological constructions that can vary with the variability of individual wills, and, in addition, the means to them can vary even when the goal is the same. Medical diagnosis surely has elements of an art given the complexity of the human body, but the general workings remain constant: no man has yet carried a child to term and delivered one, the course of life runs through the same stages except when some other mechanical event intervenes, the same or similar medicines ameliorate the same or similar illnesses except when, once again, some other mechanical event intervenes. A person who goes to see a medical doctor believes this, no matter what philosophical view that person might air.

The Cartesian doctrine, then, properly understood, admits of no qualitative distinction between thoughts, feelings, and impulses. These are one and all intelligible. Some are clear, fewer are both clear and distinct, and a great many are confused, but they are one and all thoughts. What then, must we say about our bodies insofar as they are erotic? How can eros be accounted for within the Cartesian system? In what sense can eros be regarded as mechanical? A response that is tied entirely to the sciences of biology and chemistry falls short of this unmistakable phenomenon, which puzzles everyone—from the most profound sage to the most heartsick teenager—except the very few who are not puzzled but suppose that they understand eros and/or can bring it under some control. Those people have an appropriate designation: *fool*.

What, then, becomes of the so-called Cartesian mind/body dualism? In truth, as doctrinally presented it is no duality at all, but shows itself to be a "monism" within which only quantitative differences can be discerned (if any "ism" can be regarded as appropriate). Rather, one can count to two—but with the most scrupulous care. On one side is found *res cogitans* and the twofold division within it. All else is *radically other*.

Unsurprisingly, the analogy recurs in Descartes's more precise and circumscribed formulation of "nature": "And surely there is no doubt that all I am taught by nature has some truth in it; for by 'nature,' taken generally, I understand nothing but God himself or the ordered network of created things which was instituted by God. By my own peculiar nature I understand nothing other than those things bestowed upon me by God."[3] The "or" is inclusive, embracing either God himself, the order and disposition of created things, or both. It does not embrace the things insofar as what belongs to them falls outside the idea of God and/or order and disposition, that is, outside the rational order of the universe. Thus, Descartes rejects the Aristotelian and Scholastic notion(s) of underlying substances and final causes in nature, regarding them as creations not of reason but of the lower and untrustworthy faculty of imagination. A mechanistic model consisting of efficient causes is far more in accord with the evidence and more economical as well.

Descartes offers his belief that we have probable knowledge of bodies on the basis of the argument that God could not be a deceiver. However, there is nothing in any of his arguments for the determination of probability from reason alone. We might say that our senses or our imaginations deceive us, and that reason can correct this deception by means of the sciences of arithmetic and geometry, often with the help of instrumentation that expands our ability to discern such information. One can even speak of mathematical approximations.

Probability, however, does not take its departure from reason at all, but requires sense and imagination as its initial spurs. Hume in his *Inquiry Concerning Human Understanding* has ably captured probability's strangeness:

> Here then it seems evident that when we transfer the past to the future, in order to determine the effect, which will result from any cause, we transfer all the different events in the same proportion as they have appeared in the past, and conceive one to have existed a hundred times, for instance, another ten times, and another once. As a great number of views do here concur in one event, they fortify and confirm it to the imagination, beget that sentiment which we call belief, and give its object the preference above the contrary event which is not supported by an equal number of experiments, and recurs not so frequently to the thought in transferring the past to the future. Let any one try to account for this operation of the mind upon any of the received systems of philosophy, and he will be sensible of the difficulty. For my part, I shall think it sufficient, if the present hints excite the curiosity of philosophers, and make them sensible how defective all common theories are in treating of such curious and such sublime subjects.[4]

A fissure discloses itself in the Cartesian system that has nothing to do with "mind–body dualism." The fissure is no flaw, but rather issues from the exemplary thoroughness and daring of a great thinker. What the fissure discloses in and through its depth shall be the subject matter of this book.

Leibniz

With this so-called rationalist, both substantial forms and final causes recur under modern auspices. Both Descartes and Leibniz contributed in major and lasting ways to mathematics. Descartes invented analytic geometry; Leibniz was coinventor of calculus and a major contributor to what would become formal logic. In his *Discourse on Metaphysics* (1686), he writes:

> Thus the subject term must always contain the predicate term, so one who understands perfectly the notion of the subject would also know that the predicate belongs to it.
>
> Since this is so, we can say that the nature of an individual substance or of a complete being is to have a notion so complete that it is sufficient to contain and to allow us to deduce from it all the predicates of the subject to which this notion is attributed. . . .
>
> When the proposition is not an identity, that is, when the predicate is not explicitly contained in the subject, it must be contained in it virtually.[5]

Leibniz is often credited with influencing analytic philosophy, despite the distaste for anything "metaphysical" in that orientation. One can attribute this odd interpretation to Leibniz's implicit notion that all propositions are logically necessary or, in our terms, "analytic!" This highly selective and, to my mind, unjustified and incompetent reading strips everything philosophically absorbing that the great Leibniz has to offer.

Given our finite perspective, we cannot know most individual substances completely and (most significant) deductively. Thus, from our standpoint we might know only certain facts about Alexander the Great, for example, that he was a king, a student of Aristotle, a conqueror of Darius and Poros, and so on, but "God, seeing Alexander's individual notion or haecceity, sees in it at the same time the basis and reason for all the predicates which can be said truly of him."[6] On a somewhat less exalted level, yours truly Bernie Freydberg is the husband of Akiko Kotani, the father of Malika Freydberg, is overweight by a few (several?) pounds, a Pittsburgh sports fan, and so on, all of which is contingent from a finite standpoint. But from God's perspective, all of this—including all the predicates that compose my future (oh, no!)—is beheld in a single glance.

How different is this treatment from that of Descartes? A kinship certainly obtains on one side. The universe occurs as a rational and deductive order in both thinkers. The difference on this side consists of Descartes's mathematical model and Leibniz's logical model. In neither model does anything occur that could disturb this necessary order. Both admit mechanical efficient causality into their respective systems. On the other side, one finds a sharp contrast that issues from their respective notions of substance. For Descartes, substance=being=intelligibility.

With arithmetic and geometry as the model for substance, all propositions are intrinsically identical. However, for Leibniz many if not most propositions are not intrinsically identical, but—in his language—virtually identical. There are no contingent events, but this "no" can be declared only in an ultimate sense. Thus, the notion of final cause announces its presence to account for what otherwise would be an undetermined future, or perhaps better, a future that might not follow necessarily. The name for this ultimate cause is *goodness*, which for Leibniz is inscribed in the very conception of God. But as the citation below demonstrates, "goodness," together with the famous doctrine of preestablished harmony, can indeed be thought nontheologically: "I find that the method of efficient causes, which goes much deeper and is in some sense more immediate and *a priori*, is, on the other hand, quite difficult when one comes to details, and I believe that, for the most part, our philosophers are still far from it. But the way of final causes is easier, and not infrequently of use in divining important and useful truths which one would be a long time in seeking by the other, more physical way; anatomy can provide significant examples of this."[7]

However, a fissure occurs within Leibniz's conception of goodness. This fissure, points to a gap that cannot be closed within his thought. Goodness means (1) disposition of everything in the best manner, and (2) a way of truth disclosure that is unavailable to a merely mechanical approach. Though ridiculed by Voltaire in *Candide* (more specifically, the concluding line of the *Monadology* that declared this "the best of all possible worlds"), that gifted satirist clearly lacked the kind of philosophical insight or even a competent imagination that might have led him to see how a world where outrages occur regularly might yet be seen as the best of those that are possible. That is to say, he seized cleverly but clumsily on (1) above, but missed (2) entirely.

Leibniz did not employ a Panglossian illustration that would celebrate, for example, why the suffering brought about by the Seven Years' War happened "for the best." Rather, he used the scientific work of Snellius, who discovered the laws of refraction by employing the method of final cause in seeking the "easiest" way to conduct a ray of light from one point to another, rather than the mechanical method of first determining how light was formed. In another way, the apparent "dualism" in Leibniz that issues from preestablished harmony reduces to two different methods of causal explanation within a rationally unified whole.

However, the equivocation spoken of above in the nature of goodness for Leibniz cannot be attributed to merely grammatical oversight. Between the notion of a good God who disposes all things for the best and a God who somehow provides a heuristic for scientific discovery lies a chasm. One might indeed argue along Augustinian lines that pain and even evil have no ontological status for Leibniz. However, as we will see Schelling insist later, this cannot be the case—and therefore one must concede that finitude belongs to the very idea of God in a fundamental sense. Interestingly, one can sustain the togetherness of the heuristic provision and the finite God—but only by releasing completely the idea of a perfectly good God.

Locke

Among major philosophers—and he is a major philosopher—John Locke is most frustrating. Silly arguments and rhetorical flourishes mix with crucial insights and bursts of inspiration. The power of his efforts to dismantle the Cartesian system early in the 1690 *An Essay Concerning Human Understanding* still makes itself felt in philosophy.[8] How puzzling, then, to find him affirming toward its end that all of our knowledge consists of our thinking selves, God, and the ideas of pure mathematics! The positive and enduring philosophical legacy can be found in the earlier parts of the *Essay*, and this will be my concern here.

To provide an all-too-quick survey of Locke's doctrinal opposition to Descartes, I offer the following: the Cartesian mind contains innate ideas, that is, ideas of my thinking self, God as the rational order of the universe, and the objects of pure mathematics; the Lockean mind is a tabula rasa. An idea is nothing other than what the mind should happen to be thinking about when it thinks (which is not always). All ideas come through sensation and reflection, with the latter consisting entirely of the mind's observation of its own operations. Through the latter come whatever ideas we have of self, God, and mathematics.

Early in the *Essay*, Locke stakes out a clearly militant agenda. However, these latter ideas unaccountably metamorphose into the three ideas of which we are certain and that found all others. If one were to attempt an account of this change, one might well venture the following. All three ideas are abstract ideas. That is to say, they are lifted off—ab-stracted—from sensation; further, they are abstracted from ideas of reflection that consist of our awareness of our own mental operations, for example, perception. These ideas include, among numberless others, the ideas of mathematics, as well as those of ourselves and of God.

Locke's famous distinction between primary and secondary qualities is presented in terms of the objective mind independence of the former and the subjective mind dependence of the latter. In an all-too-quick manner, this distinction is presented to students (and to ourselves) as straightforward; it takes virtually no imagination to point to a table in the classroom and give its mathematical qualities as primary and its color as secondary. In addition to these, Locke speaks of a third class of qualities, called *tertiary*, by means of which one substance acts upon another. This third class is most remarkable, as it comes neither through sensation nor through reflection.

Yet further, the Lockean notion of substance itself is most noteworthy. He "defines" it as the "I know not what" that binds the qualities together, and uses the unfortunate depiction of an unschooled Indian who supposes that the universe rests upon a large turtle, and when challenged posits a series of still larger turtles until, exasperated, he confesses that he does not know what holds up the universe. But neither, of course, does Locke.

The surrogate for Descartes's "reason" is *reflection* for Locke. Reflection does all of the work for Locke that reason does for Descartes, except for the self-guarantee of self-substantiality. However, in the ultimate sense, this self as a thinking being is reaffirmed, as are the ideas of pure mathematics. Reflection nevertheless cannot fill in the fissure disclosed by the thought of substance. Locke seems to think it as having some kind of real existence, on the ground that "something" must be joining together the various attributes of the objects of perception. This "something" must therefore be a product of reflection since it does not come through sensation but must be assumed, by inference—as existing.

Berkeley

Locke's delightfully provocative heir Berkeley fairly rejoices at disclosing the emptiness of Locke's concept of substance, and of his notion of abstract ideas by which the latter inference is drawn. *Esse est percipi* is no mere stipulation. Rather, it takes a stand for a more rigorous empiricism. This empiricism more closely circumscribes the *empeiros* that Locke addressed. Perception and being are conjoined to the exclusion of all else. Perception yields nothing like material substance, but only ideas in the mind. The distinction between primary and secondary qualities is overturned: both are mind dependent in a thoroughgoing fashion. T. S. Eliot poetized: "between the idea and the reality / falls the shadow."[9] In the earlier part of Berkeley's *Principles of Human Knowledge*, there is not so much as a shadow; or perhaps to speak more precisely, even a shadow is mind dependent and belongs to the same order as an idea.

Insofar as an idea always involves a perception, genuine abstract ideas, that is, ideas that contain no perception whatsoever, cannot take place. While we do have an idea of, for example, red that refers to any and all shades of red, this is not at all an abstract idea but what Berkeley calls a *general* idea. Every instance of red is *perceived* along with other perceptions, for example, the color red is perceived together with the perceptions of motion and of extension. Thus, the idea of red is always an experience of red, which never abstracts from all experience. The cases of motion and extension are similar. Berkeley accounts for the almost natural (though irrational) belief that we humans can possess abstract ideas to language and in particular to our capacity to speak single words, from which we draw the invalid inference that these words apply to qualities belonging to perceptions but do not, in truth, occur separately from them.

Thus, the qualities of an apple consist of its roundness, its sweetness, its crispness, its redness, and its hardness; and the qualities of a die consist of its hardness, its extension, and its figure. Subtract these qualities, and nothing remains—certainly no Lockean substance. According to Berkeley: "That the things I see with my eyes and touch with my hands do exist, really exist, I make not the least question. The only thing whose existence we deny is that which the philosophers call Matter or corporeal substance. And in doing of this there is no damage done to the rest of mankind, who, I dare say, will never miss it."[10]

Since our ideas are in the mind, to use Berkeley's terms, they are one and all passive. The stumbling block for most is the notion of spirits, which are active by contrast—and of God, the ultimate spirit. Berkeley's argument for God's existence is quite obviously indirect, and the active nature of spirits is stipulated rather than proven; that is, it looks very much like an ad hoc hypothesis to account for causal relations in the world that seem to take place quite unmistakably—except according to Berkeley's principles.

But I find Berkeley's notion of causality, when freed from the active/passive distinction, interesting and provocative. His most decisive contributions, in my view, do not reside with his criticisms of Locke or of materialism in the forms he addresses. Rather, his a-causal account of events that even surpasses Hume's in its specificity. Antecedent events are not causes, and consequent events are not effects—even when these seem obvious, such as "lightning" and "thunder" or "fire" and "heat." Rather, the first is interpreted as a sign, that is, a kind of cue or indication; the second is interpreted as what it signifies. Berkeley often refers to God as the "Author of Nature." This epithet suggests that Nature is a narration or a poem. Further clues are discernible in Berkeley's examples: "apple" contains both five letters and five qualities; "die" contains three letters and three qualities. Of course I am not suggesting a thoroughgoing numerology, but merely looking at playful hints. I am, however, suggesting that we ourselves may think in this way without ascribing the existence of nature to an active, divine poet, much less a sectarian Christian one.

Berkeley's thought, with the exception of its problematic arguments for spirits, admirably both addresses and accounts for the fissure that yawns within it and that allows for his marvelous semiotics of nature. Its outcome resembles nothing so much as a pure phenomenology if not an aesthetic interpretation of being.

Hume

That Hume is no mere precursor to Kant I have demonstrated decisively in *David Hume: Platonic Philosopher, Continental Ancestor*.[11] Here I claim that of all modern philosophers he is at once the most Socratic and, in a deep sense, the most Greek.

Regarding Hume's Socratic heritage, one need only consider the following passage from *An Inquiry Concerning Human Understanding* (1748): "The most perfect philosophy of the natural kind only staves off our ignorance a little longer: as perhaps the most perfect philosophy of the moral or metaphysical kind serves only to discover larger portions of it. Thus the observation of human blindness and weakness is the result of all philosophy, and meets us at every turn, in spite of our endeavors to elude or avoid it."[12]

Other such passages abound. Hume's skeptical conclusions, however they are interpreted, give further grounds for assigning him the rubric of Platonic/Socratic philosopher. We cannot know whether our perceptions conform to their objects. We cannot know whether they do not conform to their objects. And we cannot know whether either question concerning them makes the least sense.

Beyond this, let us reconsider his famous remark from the *Treatise of Human Nature*:

> The wretched condition, weakness, and disorder of the faculties, I must employ in my enquiries, encrease my apprehensions. And the impossibility of amending or correcting these faculties, reduces me almost to despair, and makes me resolve to perish on the barren rock, on which I am at present, rather than venture myself upon that boundless ocean, which runs out into immensity. This sudden view of my danger strikes me with melancholy; and as it is usual for that passion, above all others, to indulge itself; I cannot forbear feeding my despair, with all those desponding reflections, which the present subject furnishes me with in such abundance.[13]

On one side, Hume's "despair" images that of Socrates in the *Phaedo* before setting sail on his *deuteros plous*, his "second voyage." Socrates's search for knowledge of natural science left him utterly confused. So too did his venture into Anaxagoras's book *Nous* (*Mind*), which disappointed him in that it failed utterly to demonstrate that *Nous* ordered all things. This suggestive parallel has its limits, which makes it all the more intriguing.

In the introduction to his *Treatise*, Hume claimed to be advancing what he called "the science of man." Since this science must be more intimately connected to the human condition, the discovery of its principles should be well within reach. Like the science of nature, however, it must share the common "solid foundation" of observation and experience. As to the timing that turns the task of presenting this science in its completion, Hume traces a timeline that extends from "THALES to SOCRATES, the space of time is nearly equal to that betwixt, my Lord Bacon and some late philosophers in England, who have begun to put the science of man on a new footing."[14]

Here, one must necessarily insist that the movement from Thales to Socrates, that is, a movement from earlier to more recent, did not denote an increase in knowledge or of knowledge at all. For Socrates, the universe was not constructed of water; and he did not make a lot of money by manipulating purchases of olive presses during seasons of low prices and selling when prices were high; and there is no suggestion of his having predicted eclipses. Rather, the period in which Socrates and Plato lived culminates in the insistent proclamation of ignorance concerning those matters that most closely concern us.

Something very much the same may be said concerning Hume. Bacon is rightly celebrated for his introduction of a scientific method more encompassing, more empirically based, and ultimately more reliable than what was found in Plato or Aristotle. If it can be encompassed in a single towering principle, it would be the following: "The only hope [of science] . . . is in genuine induction."[15]

Though he seldom uses the word *induction*, Hume is rightly credited with first articulating what scholars have come to call *the problem of induction*. The latter, as is well-known, finds neither rational nor empirical justification in Hume, although we use it in "science" and in our daily lives. Hume's thoroughgoing skepticism is mitigated only by appeals to nature, which somehow rescues him from both epistemological and existential desolation. However, Hume says the following of "the skeptical philosophy": "Every passion is mortified [by such philosophy], except the love of truth; and that passion never is, nor can be, carried to too high a degree."[16] The recourse to nature, then, falls outside this love of truth, and if regarded rigorously is nothing more or other than a deus ex machina designed to account for the pleasures (and displeasures) of everyday life.

What makes Hume especially Greek, in my view, emerges in one clear sense from consideration of the outcomes of his thought, which are in reality inscribed into its beginnings. What remains after Hume's philosophical onslaught that culminates in the burning of "traditional" metaphysical texts seems to be: nothing![17] On further thought, however, one can indeed arrive at a sourcing for what Hume calls "observation" and "experience," however the scope of these two are undermined in his discourses: Chaos, which will be seen below as the withdrawn powerful origin of all things, and which occurs here as primal abyss.

Unflagging cheerfulness is the quality that bridges the Greek poetic and philosophical Muses, and it flourishes in Hume. Among all thinkers—ancient, modern, and contemporary—no one relishes the movement of his own mind as much as Hume. Even his illustration concerning the contingency of matters of fact—namely, that the "sun will rise tomorrow" is no more necessary than "the sun will not rise tomorrow"—sneaks past even the wary reader who may forget that the sun does not rise at all. Among his critics then and now, Kant came nearest to taking the full measure of Hume's philosophical work.

Kant

The thinker called "the all-destroyer" by Moses Mendelssohn (his friend!) can be viewed just as well as "the all-savior." Although Kant's critical philosophy reduced the proud name of an ontology to what he calls the humble analytic of the understanding, this analytic saved, if not elevated, the phenomena of sense. And although transcendent knowledge of the soul, the world, and God is denied to reason, the latter three ideas serve that same understanding by regulating appearances such that they are brought to the greatest possible unity.

Whether all-destroyer, all-savior, or both, the grand synthesis that is the Kantian philosophy is ultimately erected upon the same abyssal origin as those of his noble predecessors. In the *Critique of Pure Reason* it has two names, each standing in for a separate kind of absence. The first, *thing in itself* (or *things in themselves*) stands in for whatever might be utterly beyond the realm of knowing for a human being. The second, *noumenon* (or *noumena*) stands in for the nonexistent object of reason (or of the class of such objects). Subtract these absences, and rationalist metaphysics returns, with its unsolvable conundrums; so too does empiricism, with its own impenetrable *aporiai*.

It is difficult indeed to imagine primal lack with such exceptional power!

The most far-reaching declaration of darkness occurs in the all-important discussion of synthesis, all-important because Kant's questioning occurs in its terms throughout: "Synthesis in general, as we shall hereafter see, is the mere result of the power of imagination [*Einbildungskraft*], a blind but indispensible function of the soul, without which we should have no knowledge whatsoever, but of which we are scarcely ever conscious."[18] It turns out that the Pure Concepts of the Understanding (the Categories) require something more than their justification through the Transcendental Deductions. The latter secure the right of the Categories to serve as rules for appearances (i.e., for experience so limited). However, the Deduction (either A or B) cannot account for the way the Categories—which have an origin that is heterogeneous from the appearances—actually exercise their rule.

Here I must insert the following crucial note: the order of presentation in the *Critique of Pure Reason* is the opposite of the actual occurrence of the elements. Every judgment we make presupposes, in reverse order, empirical intuition, pure intuition, the Categories,[19] the Schemata, and the Principles (*Gründsätze*). The Schemata are one and all "product[s] of the imagination."[20] They are distinguished from images insofar as they provide a procedure for the generation of images. One might say, with justification, that while the Categories provide the rules for appearances, the Schemata perform the actual ruling. What about their being products of imagination? Kant writes that the Schematism of the understanding, that is, the application of the Categories to the region of sense by imagination, "is an art concealed in the depths of the human soul, whose real modes of activity nature is hardly ever to allow us to discover, and to leave open to our gaze."[21]

He proceeds to differentiate three levels within the Schematism, from most empirical to most pure. Our empirical schemata—for example, the schema of a "dog"—provide a rough guide to the "picking out" of dogs in experience. At a distance or under certain other circumstances, we might well apply this schema in error. These schemata are drawn directly from sensible experience. By contrast "the *schema* of sensible concepts, such as figures in space, is a product and, as it were, a monogram, of pure imagination, through which, and in accord with which, images themselves first become possible.... [However], they are never completely congruent with the concept."[22] On this level, the gap between concept and image, and the way imagination sustains the togetherness of concept and image, become clearer. The drawn triangle is the image of which the pure triangle in imagination is the schema.

In the case of the Categories, however, this gap fairly yawns. Pure a priori imagination neither generates nor can it generate any images of the Categories, which cannot have them by their very nature. Instead, pure intuition—time as the form of all intuition—stands in for the nonexistent images. Taking these notions together, the Categories function as the rules through which pure intuition (time) is ruled by the schemata. The four sets of Principles (*Grundsätze*) of the Pure Understanding gather these three elements into that unity whereby we can experience anything at all. Once again, this unification has always already occurred. However, as will soon be demonstrated, the Principles leave the gap even more decisively open.

One noteworthy peculiarity of this unity concerns pure intuition. In the Transcendental Aesthetic, Kant seemed to declare intuition as such to be receptive by nature, that is, to involve givenness. However, even at that early stage in his discourse a creative tension arises: intuition is said to be receptive, but pure and empirical are said to be opposite and mutually exclusive. What, then, can "pure intuition" indicate? It can only indicate an intuition that we *give ourselves*. That is to say, it seems that there must be a spontaneous aspect of pure intuition.

In a footnote to §21 of the B Deduction titled *Observation*, this spontaneity is announced in a manner unavailable earlier: "The proof of [the category providing the necessary unity of self-consciousness] rests on the *represented unity of intuition*, by which an object is given. The unity of intuition always includes in itself a synthesis of the manifold given for an intuition, and so already contains the relation of this manifold to the unity of apperception"[23] One might therefore say that there are two senses of givenness, between which an abyss dwells. This first sense concerns the synthesis of imagination whereby pure intuition always already occurs in connection with transcendental apperception. This pure synthesis provides the condition for the possibility for anything at all to occur, that is, to be given through sensation. The second sense refers precisely to the heterogeneous component of what Kant calls "representations" (*Vorstellungen*), namely, empirical intuition.

What, then, do we apprehend a priori? On one hand, we apprehend nothing apart from the connection with empirical sensation. When we suppose that we do, we find ourselves mired in transcendental illusion (immortality, freedom/natural causality, God). However, the a priori conditions for the possibility of experience can be cognized, but only in speech, that is, only in logos. These conditions consist of the Categories, the Schemata, and pure intuition (pure space, pure time) as expressed and brought to unity in the principles. One would do well to regard the principles (under transcendental apperception) as an anterior field upon which quanta flash in certain temporal patterns.

For actual apprehension to take place, something external and qualitatively unlike the field must somehow appear upon it. But what? How? What: an appearance. An appearance of what? We do not and cannot know. How? This, too, lies entirely outside our knowledge. I recall my 1973 Kant seminar at the University of Rochester with Lewis White Beck. He presented this matter to us in terms of the famous notion of the thing in itself: the thing, insofar as it is apprehended by sensation, is called a *phenomenon*. The thing, as it is apprehended by reason, is called a *noumenon*. For theoretical purposes, this term has the significance of a placeholder for a class of nonexistent things. Thus, Kant admits the noumenon only in its negative sense. The thing, regarded apart from all apprehension, is called the *thing in itself*.[24]

We can therefore say that the pure a priori component presents the criteria for anything to occur to us at all. That is, whatever can occur to us must qualify as a quantity, that is, having both an extensive and intensive magnitude; a certain time relation, that is, duration (satisfying the requirement for substantiality), succession (in a manner that satisfies the requirement for cause and effect), and simultaneity (satisfying the requirement for community). The criteria must also conform to the finite nature of the human subject, that is, to the Postulates of Empirical Thought. At this juncture one must speak in a manner that is at least somewhat oracular. What is it that can appear to us? There is no "what." There is no "is." There "is" no "being" that somehow changes or "reduces" itself to an appearance. "Being" for Kant means nothing more and nothing less than the objectivity of objects as determined by the Principles of the Pure Understanding.

The source of the empirical component also compels speech in a manner that is at least somewhat oracular—if indeed there is any sense to the problematic employment of the word "source" here. Colors, tastes, smells, and so on, like sizes and shapes, are one and all quanta. The actual quantities and the precise way they affect our sensibility are "determined" ... in the dark. While it is clear that there can be no "color in itself," it is equally clear that there can be no "triangle in itself." Red, for example, occurs at one point in the color series, just as triangle occurs as one possible figure within the scope of (for Kant) Euclidean geometry.

Thus, the entire Kantian edifice of theoretical philosophy finds itself both erected around and shaped by the crevasse to which it responds and that it preserves so creatively and uniquely.

In a different but equally intriguing manner, Kant's practical philosophy issues from gaps intrinsic to his theoretical philosophy, even as it rises above theoretical philosophy. How it does so is very much worth tracing. The gap to which I refer opens ever so slightly in the Third Antinomy, where freedom as spontaneous causality is not affirmed even as a real possibility but merely as a logical one, that is, as not issuing in a contradiction with natural causality. In the *Critique of Practical Reason*, it is affirmed without epistemological foundation—but *as itself* foundational. More specifically, freedom is asserted, that is, brought to logos in the reciprocal act whereby freedom, the *ratio essendi* of the moral law, finds its expression as the *ratio cognoscendi* of the moral law. How? It does so . . . as a free act. What can "free act" mean in this context? It can only mean a spontaneous act of imagination.

Kant attempts to distance himself from imagination in the practical critique, in the interest, one must suppose, of providing morality with a purely rational character. However, (1) the categorical imperative, both by itself and in its incarnations as the principle of nature and the principle of humanity, is synthetic, (2) the maxims for which (1) provides the measure are one and all synthetic, and (3) the application of the maxims to actual experience also involves synthesis. That is to say, imagination as the source of all synthesis drives all practical principles and activities. In my *Imagination in Kant's Critique of Practical Reason*,[25] I provide a sustained disquisition that defends this interpretation, which some have found surprising and questionable, but that still seems incontrovertible to me—based on textual evidence alone.

The abyss around which the practical critique is shaped and to which it responds could not gape any wider. For one thing, Kant writes: "It is in fact absolutely impossible by experience to discern with complete certainty a single case in which the maxim of an action, much as it may conform to duty, rested solely on moral grounds and on the conception of that duty."[26] For another thing, Kant affirms that the only aspect of the moral law we can comprehend is its incomprehensibility. Finally, one need only recall the minuscule opening that gave rise to this ungrounded towering principle. To repeat the key Kantian view, imagination is blind but indispensable, operating out of the dark.

The *Critique of Judgment* takes place beyond the scope of cognition and beyond the scope of desire (i.e., the will). Though it tempts one to find a decisive and originary linkage among all three critiques here, this temptation must be resisted. The difference in kind between the determinative judgments of the first and second critiques and the reflective judgments of the third makes such an interpretation futile. Though §9 of the *Critique of Judgment* offers what looks like low-hanging fruit insofar as it reads that the agreement of the free play of imagination with understanding is requisite for cognition in general, this says no more (but surely no less) than that this general agreement is the condition for the possibility of judgment in general—and not that the experience of beauty is so requisite. Would that all of us experienced this glorious feeling with our every step!

The "between" of the third critique occurs by virtue of distinct gaps. These gaps are listed at the end of the Introduction to the *Critique of Judgment*. There, a certain kind of feeling becomes the object of critique, namely, the feeling of pleasure and pain. This inhabits the gap between understanding on one side and desire (will) on the other. The germane "cognitive" faculty is judgment (*Urteilskraft*). In keeping with the *Critique of Pure Reason*, imagination moves unmistakably to the center (it is a "cognitive" faculty only nominally). As indicated earlier, imagination *always* dwells at the center by virtue of its synthetic function; here, however, it ascends from its home in the dark and into the light, so far as this can occur.

Its a priori principle is purposiveness (*Zweckmässigkeit*), another notion that has bedeviled Anglo-American Kant "scholars" in search of a single and consistent definition. Kant does employ it in several senses, perhaps ultimately divisible into subjective and objective purposiveness. In all cases, however, *Zweck* has the sense of "purpose" or "end"; "realm (or kingdom) of ends" translates *Reiche der Zwecke*. To gather the sense as directly as possible, *Zweckmässigkeit* has the sense of "that which accords with the measure of purpose (or end)." That Kant has more than one formulation of purpose is irrelevant to the status of the a priori principle; in fact, it serves to confirm it. Thus, the pathological pleasure one receives from anything—an ice cream cone, a Mozart string quartet—serves the purpose of providing happiness; the pathological pain one receives from gout or loss of a loved one "serves" its other side, unhappiness.

The experience of beauty, by contrast, is disinterested; that is, it does not concern natural human happiness or unhappiness and does not take into account the rational aim of morality. The experience of beauty includes the apprehension of purposiveness but without, that is, entirely apart from, all purpose—and includes nothing else. Kant famously gave priority to the beauty of nature over the beauty of art, a preference we may well question today. We might also refer to Kant's own division of applicability according to which "Art" is said to be the region of application to which the third critique points. In any case the a priori principle of purposiveness provides sufficient determinacy to guide the Analytic of the Beautiful.

The Analytic of the Sublime discloses the notion of a moral purpose (though it does not itself conclude or lead directly to this purpose) by means of two kindred excesses. The quantitative excess, according to which the notion of an absolutely great magnitude arises, has its seat in reason (and not in the understanding as in the case of beauty). The immensity of the sublime outstrips the capacity of the imagination to comprehend it. The temporary pain produced in the subject by this discord—this gap—suggests that the vocation of humanity cannot be contained in or by anything finite. The qualitative excess signals the superiority of (infinite) reason over anything finite, that is, over all nature. One might also speak of a third gap, namely, the requirement that the sublime be viewed from a position of safety, distancing the beholder from its awesome force. Like the beautiful, the sublime concerns a subjective but universal encounter for us with enormity.

Can we say, then, that Kant's aesthetic philosophy also finds itself erected around and shaped by the abyss to which it responds and that it preserves so creatively and uniquely? In a certain way, we can—but this way is distinct and distinguishable from that of the first two critiques. Reflective judgments do not and cannot occur without at least implicit determinative judgments. They concern neither the objectivity of objects nor the strictures of moral life. Rather, the gaps concerning reflective judgments are those within the subject's self-relation, upon contemplation provoked by certain kinds of implicit determinative judgment. But that is to say: upon reflection, the subject discovers a division within her/himself. In a certain way, then, the reflective judgment tracks with the Paralogisms of Pure Reason: self-knowledge is closed off in the former, while self-unity is closed off in the latter—except in those rare and treasured moments of experienced beauty.[27]

At the end of this sketch of the history of modern philosophy, I must confess that this period is the only one since the Greek era that is incontestably great. It pains me to hear both sides of today's philosophical divide make a hash of this period. However, the work is idiot-proof and bright students will be able to glean its diamonds. The garden variety Anglo-American philosophy teacher will focus on individual arguments and subject them to evaluation, often finding them wanting. No wonder, since such a teacher opines that genuine philosophy did not begin until the twentieth century which logic and natural science were recognized as its measure.

Even more painful to me is that my own tradition has recently followed the fashion of condemning this period with the all-embracing and somehow pejorative "Western metaphysics," which it holds responsible for racism, sexism, homophobia, colonialism, animal cruelty, and—for all I know—aging. The disaster of post-Heideggerian French philosophy can scarcely be overstated. Its influence has spread far and wide, to people who would not recognize the principle of sufficient reason—which they use so frequently and without any awareness—if it were a lobster that crawled up the back of their legs and grabbed hard onto their buttocks. Sadly, many people who should know better are egged on rather than restrained by the lobster's painful hold. If this history were to be taught straight and in accord with the principle of charity, as genuine love of wisdom requires, it would never cease to instruct and to inspire.

For better or for worse, it has inspired me to dare the following exploration in which I hearken to what I hear sounding from underneath the discourses of Spinoza, Schelling, and the early Nietzsche (specifically, the "Attempt at a Self-Criticism" in the second edition of the 1872 work, which he titled *The Birth of Tragedy, Or: Hellenism and Pessimism*).

Notes

1. René Descartes, *Meditations on First Philosophy*, in *Discourse on Method and Meditations on First Philosophy*, trans. Donald Cress (Indianapolis: Hackett, 1998), 100–101.
2. Ibid., 98.
3. Ibid., 97.
4. David Hume, *An Inquiry Concerning Human Understanding*, ed. Charles Hendel (Indianapolis: Bobbs-Merrill, 1977), 71.
5. Gottfried Wilhelm Leibniz, *Discourse on Metaphysics*, in *Discourse on Metaphysics and Other Essays*, trans. Daniel Garber and Roger Arieu (Indianapolis: Hackett, 1991), 8.
6. Ibid.
7. Ibid., 24.
8. John Locke, *An Essay Concerning human Understanding*, ed. Kenneth P. Winkler (Indianapolis: Hackett, 1996).
9. T. S. Eliot, *The Waste Land*, ed. Michael North (New York: W. W. Norton, 2000).
10. George Berkeley, *A Treatise Concerning the Principles of Human Knowledge*, in *George Berkeley Collection: 5 Classic Works* (New York: Waxkeep, 2013), #35.

11. Bernard Freydberg, *David Hume: Platonic Philosopher, Continental Ancestor* (Albany: State University of New York Press, 2012).
12. Hume, *Inquiry Concerning Human Understanding*, 45.
13. David Hume, *A Treatise of Human Nature*, ed. David Fate Norton and Mary J. Norton (Oxford: Oxford Philosophical Texts, 2009), 172.
14. Ibid., 4–5. Per a footnote in the book, "late philosophers" refers to "Mr. Locke, my Lord Shaftesbury, Dr. Mandeville, Mr. Hutchinson, Dr. Butler, etc."
15. Francis Bacon, "Aphorism 14," in Francis Bacon and Basil Montagu, *The Works of Francis Bacon*, vol. 14 (Philadelphia: Parry and McMillan, 1857), 32.
16. Hume, *Inquiry Concerning Human Understanding*, 43.
17. "Metaphysical," then, had two senses. One, a positive sense, referred to legitimate philosophical inquiry generally. The other, here a negative sense, referred to Scholasticism and more widely to any system of thought that could not justify its uses in *this* our world.
18. Immanuel Kant, *Critique of Pure Reason*, trans. Kemp Smith (New York: St. Martin's Press, 1965), A78, B103.
19. I leave aside the Logical Table of Judgments, since these serve as a mere clue.
20. Kant, *Critique of Pure Reason*, A140, B179.
21. Ibid., A140–141, B180–181.
22. Ibid., A142, B181.
23. Ibid., 144n.
24. Note occasional divergences; Kant occasionally slips, saying that appearances are caused by things in themselves. This could not be the case, since the category of causality refers only to appearances, that is, only to that which occurs in space and time.
25. Bernard Freydberg, *Imagination in Kant's Critique of Practical Reason* (Bloomington: Indiana University Press, 2008).
26. Immanuel Kant, *Foundations of the Metaphysics of Morals*, trans. Lewis White Beck (Indianapolis: Bobbs-Merrill, 1985), 23 (Akad. 406–407).
27. See Freydberg, *Imagination in Kant's Critique of Practical Reason*, 146.

Prelude

On Anteriority

A<small>NTERIORITY PROVIDES THE</small> guiding thread—if it may be called a thread—of this discourse. One might characterize anteriority in various ways: as primordial, as prephilosophical, as preconceptual, as prerational, as dwelling beneath, as abyss, as chasm, as underpinning undergirding, as roiling beneath, as resounding from beneath, or other such formulations. Common to all of them is the discomfort involved in apprehending their very character as well as in bringing them to language. These words—or more precisely these quasi-words—are neither concepts, nor objects, nor sensations, nor thoughts. The text that might best capture their strangeness occurs in the Heraclitean fragment: "*ho anax hou to manteion esti to en Delphois oute legei oute kruptei alla sêmainei*" (the king who prophesies at Delphi neither speaks nor conceals, but points).[1]

Schelling, who will be treated extensively in the second major section of this book, displayed extraordinary delicacy and thoughtfulness in speaking about what is anterior and what must be addressed. While his forerunner Spinoza shows no such reticence, his discourse not only presupposed anteriority, but takes place entirely within its darkly indicated horizon, located primarily in early Greek poetry and philosophy.

Anteriority, radical otherness, does not occur in Hegel's thought. In the Preface to the *Phenomenology of Spirit*, Hegel speaks of Spirit's "pure self-recognition in *absolute* otherness," which unmistakably implies that no otherness is truly absolute.[2] The progress toward Absolute Knowledge from its starting point in Sense Certainty and through the "gallery of Images" undergoes arduous labors—but no outright and permanent interruptions. The honor that ironically redounds to Hegel consists of that thinker's respect and esteem for those predecessors whom he purports to surpass.

Spinoza receives especially momentous notice, although this homage will soon be qualified: "When one begins to philosophize, the soul must commence by bathing in this ether of the one substance, in which all that one has held as true has disappeared. It is this negation of all that is particular, to which every philosopher must have come; it is the liberation of spirit and its absolute foundation."[3] According to Hegel, Spinoza never makes the journey into the particularity of oppositions within the "One Substance," though it is fair to say that if there were no Spinoza there could be no Hegel. In other words, without the concept of the One Substance, modern philosophy could not have begun in earnest. However, the thought of unassimilable anteriority does not and cannot take place in Hegelian thought. In the latter, the origin of modern philosophy occurs in Descartes: "At this point, we arrive genuinely (*eigentlich*) for the first time at philosophy of the modern (*neuen*) world and begin with Descartes. With him, we enter genuinely upon a philosophy that knows that it arises independently (*selbstständig*) from reason itself and that self-consciousness is the essential moment of the true. Here, we can say, we are at home and like sailors after a long journey (*Umgefahrt*) on the turbulent ocean can call out 'land.'"[4]

Contests in Continental philosophy abound, but one area of agreement is in the priority of *interpretation*. Logic and natural science themselves are regarded as interpretations no less than are works of art and philosophy, and reason in the strict sense (science and logic) is often seen as providing concealment and denial of truth. *A Dark History of Modern Philosophy*, a book in the Continental tradition, is certainly an interpretation as well, but along quite different lines. In this Prelude, I shall reread the Hegelian superscript in a fashion that reckons with the aforementioned unassimilable anteriority so as to expose the subsoil (and the water!) upon which it rests.

For both "home" and "land," *earth* serves as the ground. The English word *ground* bears many senses, some overlapping and some not. Ground and earth can be seen as synonymous, as can ground and land. Yet ground can also mean reason in the sense of a premise of an argument, or the basis of a belief. *Der Satz vom Grund* is translated as "the principle of sufficient reason," according to which everything that exists has a sufficient reason that it is so and not otherwise, although some of the more obscure reasons cannot be known.[5] Again, "basis" can replace earth in certain contexts, but not in others. In Greek, *hedra* has the sense of a fundament and it thus relates to ground in two senses, as well as the sense of an abode for dwelling, of a temple, and of a seat more generally. I hesitate to call this a slippage, since the shifting senses of "ground" belong to its very nature.

However, *earth* provides a somewhat different story. Earth is one of several planets belonging to one of many, many galaxies and other phenomena. Earth is the soil from which crops and vegetation grow, and the territory upon which we build our dwellings. Hesiod sings its archaic sense in his *Theogony*:

> from the beginning (*archê*), from Earth and wide Heaven bore, and the gods came into being from these, givers of good things.
>
> (*Ex archēs, hous Gaia kai Ouranos uurus hetikten, Hoi t' ek egenonto theoi, dōtēres eaōn.*)[6]

This sense antecedes the astronomical and agricultural interpretations. Unlike "ground," the latter two interpretations cover over the initiatory poetical upsurge of Earth, within which the later and narrower interpretations dwell as seeds that will later betray both their mythical and imaginative parentage.

Entreating the Muses, the poet sings:

> These things declare to me from the beginning (*ex archēs*), and tell me me which of them came first to be.... First of all (*prōtista*) Chaos (*Chaos*) came to be (*genet'*), then well-bosomed Earth, the sure foundation of all the deathless ones who hold the peaks of snowy Olympus, and dim Tartarus in the depths of the wide-pathed Earth, and Eros, most beautiful of the deathless gods, who unnerves the limbs and overcomes sense (*noon*) and wise counsels of all gods and all men within them.[7]

The Greek *Chaos* is sounded as *chasm* in English; the Greek root *is chainō*, which means "to yawn," "to gape," or "to be wide open." What does it take—what *would* it take—to think *prōtista Chaos genet'*? All efforts to translate these words into even a modest approximation of what they say run up against our senses of time, things, being and becoming. The gap between our senses and Hesiod's could hardly be greater, if indeed they are not also abysmal.

Prōtista could not mean "the first member of a series" of any kind, except from its form as a superlative. Grammar arrives long after and signals the decline of language from poetic founding to object of research. Using our best resources, we may do well to think of *protista* as qualitatively other than all that somehow issues from it. However, the "it" reference must be called into question: can we properly call *Chaos* an "it," a thing of some kind? It seems that we cannot: *Chaos* names precisely the withdrawal from "things," the withdrawal that allows for things at all. However, *Chaos* is also said to have come into being— perhaps better in this context, to have been generated. Once again, the use of the grammatical past tense does not indicate past *time*. Any division or connection with regard to being and becoming are interpolations at odds with *prōtista Chaos genet'*, which stands forth as both entirely clear and entirely enigmatic.

I venture the following English translation: "radically apart from all else has abyss come to presence." *Prōtista* does not indicate any number including one, but rather indicates originary unique otherness, radical apartness.[8] *Chaos* has nothing to do with order or disorder but rather, to borrow a Kantian trope, is the condition for the possibility of anything like order and disorder. It is a-byss, without bottom—utterly amorphous no-thing. *Genet'* is not opposed to *esti'* ("becomes" to "is," or "becoming" to "being"), but rather speaks to a sensed awareness of the abyssal, originarily other withdrawal. In this way, the language of the poet begins the preparation for our archaic rewriting of the history of modern philosophy.

Then the poet sings the invocation of amply-bosomed (*eurusternos*)— also called amply-pathed (*euruodeiēs*) Earth. Earth is both fecund and far-ranging, giving birth to and nurturing Heaven (*Ouranon*) with whom she bore many children of both peaceful and violent dispositions. The rape by Heaven of Earth begot Erebus and Night among other offspring, and also gave rise to very large Hills that served as dwelling places for the divine Nymphs. Among the children that here command the most attention are the Muses who are granddaughters of Earth, daughters of Mnemosyne (Memory) and Zeus. They are the goddesses to whom the poet appeals.

In Plato's *Phaedrus*, Eros and the Muses are the third and fourth manifestations of divine madness (the first two are prophesy and purification from past evils). In concert with the poem, the Muses do "breathe a divine voice" (30–31) into the poet, as Hesiod sings. Eros does "unnerve the limbs and overcome sense." But Socrates's account attunes these in a most decisive manner: he admits to their nonrational, perhaps destabilizing characteristic. But far from regarding this as negative, he celebrates it as *measure producing*. Of the Muses, he says that the madness of the Muses "fills the soul with a Dionysiac frenzy" (245a) and that no one who lacks this frenzy—no rational, sober human being—can hope to become an accomplished poet. And regarding Eros, "let us not be confused by any argument which tries to frighten us into believing that a man of sound mind should be chosen as friend over someone who has been stirred" (245b).

The Socratic accounts of the Muses and of Eros indicates that in the face of the coming-to-presence of the abyss, the most appropriate response—the only suitable response—is measure-producing madness. Madness in song. Madness in erotic conversation between lover and beloved. Sobriety has its place; its place is in and of the city, which comes into being out of certain needs human beings have. However, the most excessive sobriety may conceal its source in the madness that gives rise to all great things. Indeed, sobriety may be numbered among the great things, as is reason. But lurking in the depths—perhaps not nearly so far beneath the surface as one might suppose or perhaps even wish for—is the madness that gave rise to both.

I ask that this book be read as a persevering attempt to hear the music of divine madness that sounds beneath the arguments of reason, that is, as a descent into those origins anterior to analytical articulation. In other words, if *earth* is taken to mean the surface that remains surface however diligently we dig into it, then we cannot properly speak of a subsoil. We can, however, speak of and hear an echoing of what withdraws, only to make itself manifest by attending to those marvelous matters that arise out of the withdrawal: poetry, philosophy, and in an originary sense to be evinced here, nature.

Notes

1. *Sêmainei* is often rendered as "gives a sign," but this translation is a decidedly post-ancient one, and is seen as the root of "semantics." There was no such science among the Presocratics.

2. Georg Wilhelm Friedrich Hegel, *Phenomenology of Spirit*, trans. A. V. Miller (Oxford: Oxford University Press, 1977). Emphasis added.

3. Georg Wilhelm Friedrich Hegel, *Vorlesungen über der Geschichte der Philosophie* (Leipzig: Reklam, 1971), 3:299. Translations to English are the author's unless otherwise indicated.
4. Ibid., 3:250.
5. See Gottfried Wilhelm Leibniz, *The Monadology and Other Philosophical Writings*, trans. Robert Latta (London: Oxford University Press, 1925), cited in Hegel, *Vorlesungen*, 72.
6. Hesiod, *The Homeric Hymns and Homerica*, ed. Hugh G. Evelyn-White (Cambridge, MA: Harvard University Press, 1974), 45–46.
7. Ibid., 115–122.
8. F. W. J. Schelling, *Historical-Critical Introduction to the Philosophy of Mythology*, trans. Mason Richey and Markus Zisselberger (Albany: State University of New York Press, 2007), 17. I thank Jason Wirth for this reference.

2 Spinoza's Abysmal Rationalism

Concerning His Title and Related Matters

Ethics is a word that has assimilated so thoroughly into our everyday vocabulary that its sense as well as its origin has virtually dissipated. It can refer indifferently to moral principles, to rules of conduct generally, to aspects of character, and to an individual's personal set of preferred values. Buried beneath these senses is the original Greek *ēthos*, which signified place of habitation or dwelling place. One can locate this latter sense in the Heraclitean Fragment that reads: *ēthos anthrōpō daimōn*.[1] In another careless assimilation that has found its way into presumably learned literature, G. S. Kirk, J. E. Raven, and M. Schofield translate "a man's character is his destiny," a bromide that appears in frames in the offices of many who have neither knowledge nor interest in its distant source.

One of Heidegger's least controversial and most illuminating translations occurs in this passage in the *Letter on Humanism* (1946): "The human being dwells in the nearness of god" (*Der Spruch sagt: der Mensch wohnt, insofern es Mensch ist, in der Nähe Gottes*).[2] This translation is at once more in tune with the ancient Greek, more literal, and at the same time more mythical. That is, a certain opacity belongs to its very saying. The only word of the three that appears to be clear is *anthrōpō*. It can only be translated as "man" or "human being." By contrast, later meanings of *ēthos* do devolve and shade into the other senses indicated above.

The usage in Greek that best exemplifies this slippage is Aristotle's *Ethikōn Nikomacheiōn*, or *Nichomachean Ethics*. This book putatively serves as a manual intended for the author's son Nichomachus as a guide to the best life for a human being, though the latter's name appears nowhere in it. If one were to attempt to reach back for traces of the originary sense of *ethōs*, the access is difficult but not wholly impassable. The telos, or end, of the good life is said to be happiness, *eudaimonia*—a word in which *daimōn* clearly sounds. The elements of Aristotelian *eudaimonia* also can recollect the originary sense of *ethōs*, as will be discussed shortly.

The way back is more within reach in Plato, for whom mythos and logos are not yet separate. The *Republic*, for example, begins at a site full of mythical associations: Piraeus. One of the mythoi identifies Piraeus as an entranceway by which the souls make their way to Hades. Regarding Hades, the remainder of Book I has references to this place and to the god whose name it bears.³ The sense of *daimōn*—again literal and also mythical—is, first of all, god. Its twofold originary sense shines forth in the myth of Er with which Plato's *Republic* concludes. According to what will become an important myth in this Spinoza interpretation, Lachesis—the daughter of Necessity—directs the souls that have arrived in Hades to begin "their new death-bringing cycle for the mortal race. A *daimōn* will not select you, but you will choose a *daimōn*.⁴ Let him who gets the first lot make the first choice of a life to which he will be bound by necessity (*anagkē*). Virtue is without a master; as he honors or dishonors her, each will have more or less of her. The blame (*aitia*) belongs to him who chooses; the god is blameless (*anaitios*)."⁵

This passage perches on the cusp of ancient and modern, and is reducible to neither. The blamelessness of the god coheres well with the Spinozist conception, but the apparently polytheistic presupposition (though it occurs in a mythical context) clearly does not, nor does the aspect of "choice." But this does not cut to the core of the requirement for a reinscription of Spinoza in the history of modern philosophy. One finds it both more peculiarly and more strikingly adumbrated in the sense of *aitia* in the passage. The "normal" translation as *cause* would render the passage: "The cause belongs to him who chooses; the god is causeless [or: without cause]," which makes no sense in this (or any) context. The verb *aitiaomai* is Homeric, and has the sense of "blame." A most interesting instance occurs in *Iliad*, where Paris answers brother Hektor's denigration of him in this way: "Hector, since your spirit blames me though blameless [*anaition aitiasthai*]" (XIII, 775). *Aitia* as *cause* did not belong to this vocabulary, and did not find its way into use in our sense at all until Plato, and did not enter a systematic philosophical vocabulary until Aristotle. The rethinking of the Latin *causa* back to this myth-related Greek sense of *aitia* will play a key part in this rewriting.

How, then, is the beginning of the *Ethics* to be heard? First of all, the full title is *Ethica ordine geometrico demonstrata* or *Ethics demonstrated in geometrical order*. Here is a retranslation of each word into Greek, which Sallis calls a "countertranslation,"⁶ as it recovers the originary power of words: *ethica*:: *ethōs*; *ordine*:: *sustēma*; *geometrico*:: *geo+metron*; *demonstrata*:: *apodeiknumi*, that is, *apo+deiknumi*. In English: neighborhood, nearness or dwelling; system or standing-together; geometrical or earth + measure; demonstrate or show from. The full title gathers these words into a unity. From *ethōs*: nearness; from *ordine*: system; from *geometron*: taking the measure of earth; from *apodeiknumi*: demonstrating as showing forth.

The last word provides the crucial bridge here. *Apokeiknumi, apodeixis*, is strongly affiliated with mythos in Plato's *Phaedrus*. Socrates characterizes his great myth on eros as an *apodeixis* that the clever (*deinois*) will not trust (*apistos*), but that the wise (*sophois*) will trust (*pistē*) (245c1–2). It is, of course, clear that Spinoza's text operates according to reason, and that at least for the most part, the terms he employs are understood to function rationally. A "demonstration" in his understanding is a "rational proof," at least strongly along the lines of the proofs in Euclid's *Elements*. Our journey here attempts to take us to a region anterior to the thought of reason, to that Platonic-choric "place" out of which all concepts sprang as its children.

God

In this interpretation, which will justify itself fully as the discourse proceeds, God is anteriority—unconditionally, absolutely, exclusively. God, or Nature, must be conceived. With some allowance for a language that must remain nebulous due to the dark and difficult matter it attempts to address, reason is the surface of which God's anteriority is the depth. Spinoza, and Schelling after him and whom he inspired, committed themselves to the articulation of a system such that a single principle serves as the source from which all of its offshoots are derived. In this context, how should we hear the word "principle?" Is it to be heard as *Grundsatz*, as it sounds in Kant, Fichte, and Hegel? Or as *Prinzip*? Or rather as abounding with resonances that draw from sources both ancient and modern?

Spinoza's thought serves an axial function for philosophy because (1) it enshrines reason as the appropriate means of seeking truth and living a good life, and (2) at the same time, it releases language from its strictly rational sense and, in so doing, directs attention at once to its secreted ancient resonances. Thus, when we attempt to conceive of God, we must also somehow catch hold of God's abysmal anteriority, that is, as the qualitatively concealed antecedent of itself. This is why his thought most closely aligns itself with his Greek forebears who pondered first matters long before Euclid wrote.

The God of Spinoza's *Ethics* might seem to take its departure from a notion that has little or nothing in common with early Greek thought. Neither Heraclitus's god that is "day night, winter summer, war peace, satiety hunger,"[7] nor Parmenidean oneness (Parmenides never speaks of one god, only of the goddess of Night and Day, and of the Sun god), nor of Socrates in the *Apology* who speaks of a god who alone is wise and, toward the *Apology*'s end, of gods who are ever mindful of good in human beings. In what sense, if any, can we say that the austere Spinoza was a closet polytheist? In our terms, he was neither a theist nor a polytheist— nor, for that matter, was he an atheist.

He was accused of that "heresy" and excommunicated as a result, and many still regard him as an atheist—although this no longer provokes such excessive self-righteousness. Spinoza's God may seem, however, to have its immediate predecessor in Descartes's God of the *Discourse on Method*. There, Descartes likens the certainty of God's existence to certainty that the sum of the three angles of any triangle are equal to two right angles—only that the existence of God is, if anything, even more evident.[8] This account is usually taken to be a version of the ontological proof for the existence of God, as is Spinoza's. I say that this is mistaken, and that the absence of such language, which was clearly available to both, shows that it was not such a proof.

Rather, to understand God in Spinoza's system requires what will later be called *intuition*, an instantaneous unmediated leap that exceeds syllogistic reasoning in every way. First, intuition does not take place in time, but in the realm of eternity. Beyond both empirical matters and formal-logical reasoning, intuition brings the human mind into union with God and God's attributes and modes insofar as these admit of access. "Beyond," however, cannot be restricted to what might metaphorically be called an "upward" movement. Intuition does not bring one to a "higher" plane or to any plane at all. Concomitantly, intuition delivers one to another heterogeneous region, through the crevasse opening to the unfathomable nether portion of which the ancient Greeks sang.

In the eternal aspect, Spinoza's God could not have acted in any other way. There is simply no free will; there is none in God, and none in us. God did not so love man, and so forth, because God does not love; nor does God hate sin, since God does not hate. Human love of God has a major place for human beings, but this love does not resemble adoration or gratitude. Rather, it requires the action of the human intellect as it grasps the essence of God in one intuition. Matters in the subterrestrial aspect occur in dissonant concert with the eternal aspect. God is neither outside the world nor in the world. Rather, God must be thought of as that anteriority in terms of which all "inside" and "outside" can occur at all.

Both Parmenides and Heraclitus are direct if distant ancestors of Spinoza. First, Heraclitus: "Listening not to me but to the *logos*, it is wise to agree that all being is one" (*Ouk emou alla tou logou akousantas homologein sophon estin hen panta einai*).[9] All oppositions refer back to that which is one and the same. Reference to Parmenides's so-called monism pertains to Spinozism clearly but at a distance. Spinoza's language, however, carries unmistakable echoes despite its rationalist garb: "I say that to the essence of any thing belongs that which, being given, the thing is . . . also necessarily posited and which, being taken away, the thing is necessarily . . . taken away; or that without which the thing can neither be nor be conceived, and which can neither be nor be conceived without the thing."[10]

I try to listen thoughtfully to the words of Parmenides:

> just one *mythos* of a way is left, that it is (*hōs estin*): on this way the signs (*sēmat'*) are many, such as being uncreated (*agenēton*) and imperishable (*anōlethron*) it is (*estin*), whole, of a single kind (*mounogenes*) and unshaken (*atremes*) and complete (*teleion*).[11]

One can discern their unmistakable undercurrent beneath Spinoza's discourse, as there can be only one such thing for Spinoza: God. Every "characteristic" of *estin* sounded in Parmenides's mythos also serves in the rationalist language of predication for Spinoza.

How may mythos be thought in this context? The thought overlaps with one of the lexicographic senses of logos, namely, something that is said, or word—word of mouth. It is not identical with the Heraclitean sense of logos, which *can* be thought of in our terms as gathering-in-one. In his *An Introduction to Metaphysics* (*Einführung in die Metaphysik*), Heidegger makes a major contribution to the interpretation of these two Presocratic thinkers when he writes: "Parmenides stood on the same ground as Heraclitus. Where indeed would we expect these two Greek thinkers, the inaugurators of all philosophy, to stand if not in the Being of beings? For Parmenides, too, Being was *hen* [one], *suneches*, [i.e.,] holding together in itself, complete and fully-standing."[12]

Heraclitus and Parmenides stood on the same ground: "the thinking of Parmenides and Heraclitus was still poetic, which in this case means philosophical and not scientific."[13] However, standing on the same ground, in the radiance of Being out of which all appearing can occur at all, they spoke differently. Parmenides's mythos consisted of one word—or more precisely, Parmenides's mythos (word) is one: *estin*, which we render as "it is." All else serves only to illuminate *estin*. For his perhaps unconscious descendant, the same holds for Spinoza's God: "From the necessity of the divine nature there must follow infinitely many things in infinitely many modes (i.e. everything that can fall under an infinite intellect)."[14]

The definition of God as a substance consisting of absolutely infinite attributes, each of which expresses eternal and infinite essence, presents a thought such that the seams of the Spinozist system threatens to fray. Definition—de-finition: what if we treat this word as a concept in the manner that Spinoza treats other primal concepts? In that case, the concept of definition would include the setting of limits in accord with its essence. In the definitions presented, this is indeed the case. But the definition of God exceeds definition itself. The ascription of infinitude and eternality escapes the framework within which the concept of God acquires its sense.

How must this excess be thought? How can a definition include infinitude and eternality? It can do so only if an anterior influence exercises itself silently but powerfully upon the definitions. This is the poetic notion of Necessity, the necessity that lurks in the depths, that undergirds Spinoza's "Definitions." That is to say, the rational system Spinoza proposes emerges from a dark source that can be neither seen nor directly confronted.

Necessity

The much-discussed notion of necessity in philosophy usually occurs as a counter concept to freedom. Spinoza's account owes nothing to this discussion. Rather, freedom and necessity are inextricably intertwined: "That thing is called free which exists solely from the necessity of its own nature alone, and is determined to act by itself alone. A thing called necessary, or compelled, which is determined by another to exist and to produce an effect of a certain and determinate manner."[15] "In nature there is nothing contingent, but all things have been determined from the necessity of the divine nature to exist and produce an effect in a certain way."[16]

Spinoza's thought situates itself at the crux of Greek and modern thought in a singular manner. But this situation breaches the only apparent divide between ancient and modern. In one sense, it occurs quite properly within the chronological as well as the thematic account of the history of modern philosophy. It enshrines the life lived in accord with reason as the best and the happiest life. Efficient causality becomes the way of studying and describing natural processes. The supernatural is banished from the latter study and description. In another, it emanates from the primordial underworld of which the Greek poets sang.

First, from the side of modern philosophy, equivocations in the Cartesian philosophy no longer obtain. In Descartes, the twofold of *res cogitans* and *res extensa* becomes a "onefold": *cogito ergo sum* becomes God's necessary existence and the latter twofold becomes two separate modes, the only modes of God's infinite modes known to us. Most tellingly, Descartes's division between the will and the intellect is canceled: "Will and intellect are one and the same thing."[17]

For Descartes, freedom belongs to, even constitutes the essence of, the human will. The range of this freedom is infinite, imaging the divine will in its fashion. However, whereas the divine will is infallible, the human will is the source of error when it exceeds the clear and distinct ideas conceived by the intellect. This reconfiguration of freedom constitutes the most radical of Spinoza's appropriations of Descartes. Just as God and nature become identical, and just as substance becomes one instead of two, freedom and necessity are one and indistinguishable. Here is the site at which Spinoza's thought reaches back to the Greeks as well as forward to both the moderns and to certain thinkers closer to our own time, such as Einstein. According to Spinoza, "Will cannot be called a free cause, but only a necessary one."[18]

For much of modern thought, at least through Kant, Spinoza's notion of freedom of the will proved to be unassimilable. The major British empiricists Locke, Berkeley, and Hume each argued for the "liberty" of the will; for Leibniz after Descartes, freedom belongs to every individual action. Kant's third antinomy established the possibility of freedom as spontaneous causality. That is, the necessary order of efficient causality may remain undisturbed by the freedom of the subject. In Kant's moral philosophy, the reality of freedom is actually identified as the will; freedom takes the form of obedience or disobedience to the moral law in its several formulations. None of the above treatments directly address Spinoza's conception of freedom of the will.

Kant's critical philosophy shared a common trait with Spinoza's thought that would inspire the great movement called German Idealism. Like the critical philosophy, Spinoza's thought is systematic, that is, the thought of both derives from a single highest principle in terms of which all its parts are thoroughly determined. In the Introduction to the *Critique of Practical Reason*, Kant writes:

> But still another thing must be attended to which is of a more philosophical and architectonic character. It is to grasp correctly the idea of the whole, and as united in a pure rational faculty. This examination and the attainment of such a view are obtainable only through a most intimate acquaintance of the system. Those who are loath to engage in the first of these inquiries and who do not consider acquiring this acquaintance worth the trouble will not reach the second stage, the synoptic view, which is a synthetic return to that which was previously given only analytically.[19]

However, the concept of freedom is never derived but presupposed. It is the one fact of reason, according to Kant; but facts appear nowhere on his epistemological map. Freedom is not an object, or even a subject, of knowledge. Freedom functions as the highest principle of the Kantian philosophy, and properly so. It grounds both the practical philosophy, which has primacy, and the theoretical philosophy. Freedom provides fundamental inspiration for the thought of Fichte, Schelling, and Hegel.

However, there is no place for these various conceptions of freedom in the thought of Spinoza, for whom the unfolding of things takes place inexorably and could not conceivably be otherwise. Spinoza's comments on moral valuation could hardly differ more from Kant's. For the latter, moral principles admit no admixture with anything empirical. By contrast, for Spinoza, "Knowledge of good and evil is nothing other but the emotion of pleasure or pain insofar as we become conscious of it."[20] This matter ultimately exceeds the scope of this discourse, but can be addressed sufficiently in the following manner: for Spinoza, there simply can be no transcendent or transcendental principle. The immanence of all things in God or Nature is a principle so inviolable that any thought of an "existing outside" or "other" is thoroughgoing nonsense. For example, the notion of final cause, which has a long and controversial but honorable philosophical pedigree, finds Spinoza mocking it as food for the weak and stupid.

The force of the Kantian concept of freedom can be seen not only in its direct influence on Kant's successors. It also stands as a towering contribution to the progress of human history. Its formulation as the principle of humanity reads: treat humanity, in your own person and in that of others, only as an end and never as a means only. As is well-known, Kant's views of gender and race are odious by contemporary standards. But these contemporary standards have been significantly shaped by the principle of humanity, which far transcends its time.

From the ancient side, however, nothing like such a principle can be found in the poetry of the Greeks, and the latter area shall prove decisive here. Nor can its salubrious effects be found in Spinoza. The power and sway of poetry for the classical Greeks and their forebears eclipsed the kinds of moral concerns that occupied the moderns. The Homeric epics are unique in their unity of imagination and rigor. In them, one finds the most enraptured melody within a fixed structure; one finds convincing narrative among impossible events. Within the calm musical surface dwells the most graphic cruelty. The extant ancient Greek tragedies and comedies have no modern counterpart either in terms of music or of depth.

In the tragedies, iron necessity rules.[21] The contemporary poet Gjertrud Schnackenberg is its particularly gifted singer. She fully feels and articulates the nature and power of necessity. Consider these lines from the first part of *The Throne of Labdacus*, she sings of the source of the *Oedipus the King* tale, which the god is about to set to music:

> A story like a Sphinx-dictated riddle
> Even the god can't solve
>
> A story sent by the god
> By Faceless Necessity
>
> Who held a clay tablet up
> To the bandaged eyes

Of a Bound Man
Playing his harp with his feet
The most archaic tablet
Merely a copy of a still more archaic tablet
The long-broken, unrecoverable original
First sent to him, the earliest tablet
With a story about a nameless foundling
Lost on the mountainside of his own life,
Written, not in Greek, but in the language
Of the Gods.

Parmenides's Necessity (*Anagkē*) throbs beneath Spinoza's. So too does Heraclitus's, but in a somewhat different register: in Heraclitus, the word *Anagkē* or any variant of it does not occur. Rather, *chrē* is Heraclitus's word that is customarily translated in terms of the necessary. (This word also occurs first in Parmenides Fragment 293, which begins: *chrē to legein te noein t' eon emmenai: estin gar einai.*[22]) Kirk, Raven, and Schofield render it "What is there to be said and thought must needs be."[23] It is clear that they are attempting to capture the sense of this difficult sentence by ordering its words in a grammatical fashion. Heidegger locates the key to the passage at its end, from the *eon emmenai*, which he hears as the Being of beings within which all responsiveness is moved to occur.[24] Further, his rendering of *nous* locates undertones that can be heard beneath its traditional interpretation as "thought" or "intellection": *noein*, from the verb *noeō*, also means heart, taking to heart. And in *Being and Time*, he calls attention to another originary sense, namely, perception, even "perception with the eyes."[25] Interpreting *chrē* as "it is useful"—the German is *Brauch*—is once again in keeping with the saying in which *legein* and *noein* are delivered to the *eon emmenai*.

But Parmenides's *Anagkē* must be heard otherwise. The last sentence of Fragment 298 reads:

> The same (*tauton*) and in the same (*en tautō*) it lies on its same (*heauton*) and thus fixed it will stay. For strong Necessity (*Anagkē*) has it imprisoned (*desmoisin*) in a limit (*peiratos*) that keeps it confined within.[26]

How is "strong Necessity" to be heard here? Is there a "weak" or a "moderate" Necessity from which it is distinguished? Further, does the above imply an "outside," perhaps a region of freedom belonging to *estin* as *tauton* but denied it by *Anagkē*'s stronghold? None of the above: Parmenidean Necessity must rather be heard in terms of its *anteriority* to any matters that the aforementioned questions presuppose. Necessity's imprisonment of *estin* as *tauton* must be heard as its *gift*. Through its gift of its imprisonment of Being, Being may draw the thought of those under its sway toward it.

Parmenides's *Anagkē* recalls what we inappropriately call the personification as the goddess, the one whose daughters are the three Moirai (Fates) of Lachesis, Clōthō, and Atropos. If we allow the mythos to serve as the proper context, *Anagkē* was present at the creation of the cosmos, and is without parents. That is to say, *Anagkē* dwells radically outside *any* causal connection. However, her "spouse," Chronos, also present at the birth of the cosmos, also without parents, hence also beyond cause and effect, receives no mention in the Fragments available to us. Indeed, it would be difficult to see where he could find a place in Parmenides's mythos. For Chronos—Time—as the god who eats his children until chained by his son Zeus, at least seems to signal ongoing change, that is, coming into being and passing away. For Parmenides, the latter is the way of falsehood. When his discourse moves from matters of *nous* (one, thought) to matters of *aisthesis* (many, sensation), he writes according to Simplicius:

> Here I pause from my trustworthy *logos* (*piston logon*) and thought concerning truth (*alētheia*); the opinions (*doxas*) of mortals learn, hearing the deceitful ordering of what I say (*epeōn*).[27]

What can be said concerning logos in light of the above ventures into the fragments of Heraclitus and Parmenides? The well-known translation into "reason" in the Middle Ages has shaped all philosophy since. *Reason* has proved to be the focal point of all philosophy, even recent Continental philosophy in which it has become something of a pariah. Therefore, "reason" cannot be called a merely arbitrary rendering. If it were merely arbitrary, how could it have exercised such thoroughgoing influence and power? It is, after all, the engine of science and technology, according to most, as well as the notion responsible for repression of many kinds to some.

Nevertheless, as a translation it is an *interpretation*, albeit a most fateful one. How can one oppose reason, except by rational means? (Hume noted the irony of this in his own philosophy.) In my language,

I have elsewhere called reason a "ruling image," and its principal offshoots, for example, space, time, the categorical imperative, "ruling images." The basis for this language can be found in that aspect of Socratic ignorance according to which we are closed off radically from knowledge of originals. Within the image-play that determines how we live and move, some of the images serve and/or can serve as anchors. These are the ones I call ruling images. Logos rules with extraordinary scope.

One can say, for example, that in Heraclitus the logos unifies opposites such as living/dead and waking/sleeping. However, it seems clearly inappropriate to regard living and dead or waking and sleeping, for example, as first being separated and only then as brought together in or by the logos. In an analogous manner, Parmenides's logos in his *chrē to legein te noein t' eon emmenai* speaks to its gathering with thought in their address of Being, and the logos in his *logon piston* (trustworthy logos) receives its trustworthiness precisely from its bond to the one truth of Being. The anteriority of logos as reason in Spinoza and the anteriority of God are one.

Interlude on Necessity and Causality

Among Spinoza's "Definitions" at the outset of his *Ethics*, every one of the key concepts from which he will develop his system can be found—except two principal ones. There is no definition for *necessity*, at least for the primordial necessity from which his thought unfolds, nor is there any definition of *cause*, the way of necessity's unfolding. Rather, every definition presupposes them both, that is, presupposes that things can never be other than they are and can never be in any other manner than they are. For example, in Part I, Definition 1, the existence of a self-caused being is included in the essence of a self-caused being, that is, the concept of "self-caused being" *necessitates* "existence."[28] Substance is (by definition) in itself, that is, it provides its own support, and hence necessarily requires only itself, that is, it "does not require the conception of anything else" to be formed (Definition 3).[29] The attributes and modes of substance (Definitions 4 and 5) are augmentations of the definition of substance.[30] In the second section of this rewriting, when Schelling takes up Spinoza, these augmentations are creatively appropriated. The twofold of thought and body *necessarily* presupposes that only within the realm of each can there be limits upon them (Definition 2).[31]

The discourse on necessity in Plato's *Timaeus* provides the dissonant concert for Spinozist necessity. In the *Timaeus*, this discourse constitutes a second beginning. This second beginning culminates in what John Sallis called a chorology, a logos of the *chora*. Unlike the discourse issuing from *nous* that separated being from becoming and demonstrated that the cosmos belongs in the realm of becoming, the discourse from necessity "sets things adrift," that is, it interrupts the first discourse and undermines it. Though the discourse from necessity appears much later than the discourse from *nous*, necessity is present from the outset of the first discourse, making the first discourse possible. Necessity compels a "compromise" with *nous*; this compromise might also be called a capitulation. Were it not for the "disclosure" of the *chora*—also called "receptacle" and "nurse of becoming"—in the discourse of necessity, there could be no appearing at all of any kind and certainly no way to discriminate being and becoming.

"Disclosure" must be written within quotation marks because it is just as much a nondisclosure. The *chora* is seen only obscurely and with great difficulty; its apprehension, if that word is appropriate, occurs as if in a dreamlike image within a dream. It "never shows its own face," although all showing requires it. It can be said to withdraw for the sake of showing, so long as one does not attach causal significance to this withdrawal. This absence of causal significance marks the crucial difference between Plato's ancient account of necessity and the account that we find in every philosopher from Descartes through Hegel.

However, oddly pronounced echoes occur. I say "oddly" because these resonances issue from an *absence*. Just as we do not *see* the necessity spoken of in the *Timaeus*, we cannot see necessity at work in causality either. Locke alone among modern philosophers attributed this "shortcoming" to the grossness of our organs of sensation. In Spinoza, it seems that we can surely *think* necessity as it occurs in the definitions. However, upon closer inspection this apparent obviousness may prove more elusive than suspected. Definition 1 asserts that a self-caused being is one "whose essence involves existence, *or* whose nature cannot be conceived except as existing."[32] Rather than being a restatement of the so-called ontological proof, it is something more and other, namely, a delimiting—a drawing of limits between—self-caused beings from "other-caused" beings. To be sure, as a proof, it has a history within which Spinoza works. However, his does not call it a proof but a definition, a setting of limits.

As does necessity, the modern notion of causality moves to the center of Spinoza's discourse. But how must *cause* be heard and thought? Spinoza appropriates the language of Scholasticism, although his doctrines would and did alarm theologians of all religions. However, Aquinas's translations into Latin of the causes as stated in Aristotle's *Physics* are laden with interpretations that have so forcefully entered modern philosophy that full excision remains impossible, at least at this time. This archaic reinscription should be seen as an early but sustained effort to weaken their hold.

In Plato's *Phaedo* at 96a, Socrates speaks retrospectively of a "marvelous" (*thaumastos*) "wisdom" (*sophias*) he sought as a younger man that seemed "glorious" (*huperēphanos*) at the time.[33] This wisdom concerned "causes" (*aitiai*), and would supply answers to the "why" or "through what" (*dia ti*) of how each being came to be. The result is well-known, and strictly speaking does not answer the original question at all. Socrates's "simple" (*euethês*) decision is for the *eidos*, which directs itself to the participation of beings and not to the way they come into being in nature. Thus, why, or through what, is a woman tall? She participates in the *eidos* tallness. Why is this person a woman? Similarly, this person participates in the *eidos* womanness. *Eidos* is derived from *eidenai*, which means "to have seen." *Eidenai* is the past participle of *horaō*, to see. As John Sallis so crucially observed, *eidos* refers to a way of seeing, and not to another and/or special class of object.

Socrates's biggest disappointment issued from reading Anaxagoras's book *Nous*, which he hoped would tell him how all things were designed for the best. What he found instead was what we would call a mechanical conception of intellect. It would account for Socrates's presence in prison in terms of his bones and their placement, rather than the best judgment of the Athenian court and his judgment that it was best to remain imprisoned rather than to escape. In modern language, Socrates sought the explanation of why the cosmos and all things in it were best disposed, which he never doubted. However, his search for a causal account proved entirely disappointing.

Accurate translations of the four Greek *aitiai* as they occur in Aristotle's *Physics* would be close to the following: *hule*—that from which (*to ex ou gignetai*); the *eidos* and the *paradeigma*—that into which; *hê archê tês metabolês hê tês hê protê ê tês erêmêseôs*—that which initiates change or rest; *to heneka, to ou heneka*—the end or purpose, that for the sake of which something is done.[34] These were rendered—and I say misrendered—as "material cause," "formal cause," "efficient cause," and "final cause," respectively, by Thomas Aquinas.[35] In these terms, it seems that Socrates sought the "final cause" but gave up on that search, leading him instead to institute "a *methodos* of my own titled *eike phuros* (random mixing)." By contrast, Aristotle gave pride of place to "final cause," though the same entity could come about through more than one cause.

Spinoza's first definition of Part I: Of God, concerns the difference between self-caused and implied "other-caused" beings. Before one can make sense of this definition and others that turn on "cause," we must look for a suitable location in Spinoza's account. The one that most strongly suggests itself is found in Scholium 2 of Proposition 9, according to which "Every substance is necessarily infinite." In its midst, Spinoza gives four statements that, in his words, it "must be noted":[36]

(1) The first concerns the nature of definition includes "nothing beyond the thing defined," e.g., triangle is defined as three-sided polygon.
(2) The second cannot concern "a fixed number of individuals," e.g., hence no specific number of triangles can be included in the definition of triangle.
(3) "For each individual existent thing there must necessarily be a cause for its existence."
(4) The aforementioned cause in (3) must either belong to the nature of the thing, or be independent of the thing.

In terms of the so-called four Aristotelian causes, (1) and (2) address what would be called the formal cause. What might be called "Spinozist Logic" is presented in his offering of two "impossible" images "trees and stones as well as men being formed from seeds." Such people are confused and are unaccustomed to know things through their primary causes or how they are produced. Regarding (3) and (4) above, the only two kinds of causes that are admissible are those that have come down to Spinoza as efficient cause or as formal cause. The key to this logic rests upon the uncreated nature of substance; or, in the language with which we here wrestle, the self-caused nature of substance. But anterior stirring abides beneath its rational surface.

Imagination

To behold "God or Nature," it would seem, requires the suppression of the human imagination. Doctrinally speaking, the human imagination is a function of the human body, just as memory is. But read carefully, the fragmented result of human imagination in inventing final cause in harmony with human aspirations—the *figment-character* of final causality—constitutes its objectionable aspect. As we will see later, imagination in another guise performs an essential function for the human mind. For now, we can only say that the questionable freedom of the human imagination—one might call it the *arrogated* freedom—leads human beings to orient themselves toward an impossible object, toward contingent existence that is nonexistence in reality.

In hearing this, we also hear Heraclitus on how *hoi polloi* believes that each of its members follows its own insight rather than the logos common to all. And we also hear Parmenides on the way of Being bound by strong Necessity as the way of truth as differentiated from the "backward-turning" way of mortals who are guided by opinion.[37] To suppose that things could be—or should be—other than they are is folly and weakness according to Spinoza; according to his pre-Socratic Greek forebears, saying this transgresses the appropriately human limits, that is, it is an instance of hubris.

Returning briefly to what I have been calling the doctrinal aspect of the *Ethics*, what can be said more precisely concerning the suppression of imagination? In *Force of Imagination*, John Sallis speaks of "how Descartes repeatedly struggles to restrain the force of imagination and to restrain himself from relying on it."[38] In Spinoza's rescission of the twofold of *res cogitans* and *res extensa* in Descartes, one might suppose that the tension of which Sallis speaks relaxes entirely. Human imagination seems to be coordinated with folly; only reason provides the way to wisdom, the way to appropriate dwelling. Human imagination parts company radically with reason.

In the opening paragraph of Descartes's *Discourse on Method*, reason or "good sense" is defined as "the power of judging well and of distinguishing the true from the false."[39] In his *Principles of Cartesian Philosophy*, Spinoza understands his project as placing Descartes's thought into a mathematical style like the one found in the *Ethics*, that is, as a series of definitions, axioms, postulates, corollaries, and so forth. By studying his treatise on Descartes next to the *Ethics*, the stark consequences of their difference becomes clear. Reason is not so much as mentioned in Part I, and does not receive any treatment at all until the human mind becomes the subject of inquiry. Even there, reason is not given primary importance. As is well-known, Spinoza speaks of three kinds of knowledge: the lowest, opinion and imagination, the second as what we would call reason, and the third or highest as intuition. Even a brief consideration of Spinoza's three kinds of knowledge in Part II of the *Ethics*, Proposition 40, establishes the view I offer here. Knowledge of the first kind, called "opinion" or "imagination," is the only kind that admits of the possibility of falsehood. Knowledge of the second kind, involving "common notions and adequate ideas of the properties of things," is called "reason." The second kind of knowledge resembles Cartesian knowledge most closely. The distinction between them, at once subtle and sharp, manifests itself in Spinoza's third kind of knowledge, which does not occur (except in the faintest traces and only in retrospect), in Descartes's thought.

The third kind of knowledge "proceeds from an adequate idea of the formal essence of certain attributes of God to an adequate knowledge of the . . . essence of things."[40] Spinoza's "illustration" is the following: Given the problem of finding the fourth number of the proportion $1 : 2 :: 3 : x$, the "tradesman" can multiply the fractions and arrive at the correct result by means of reason, while the much more sapient person can see immediately that 6 is the solution. How is this to be thought in connection with his first definition, and with his first mention of God within the first group of definitions?

Following the illustration, a tradesman can presumably follow the reasoning according to which existence is deduced from self-causation just as unmarried is deduced from bachelor or $A = ½bh$ is deduced from (Euclidean) triangularity, just as many students (and professors like us!) present this as a syllogistic version of the ontological proof with the minor premise implicit. But Spinoza considers intuition to be beyond "tradesman-knowledge." In this sense, Definition 1 requires *no inference*. It is given to the thinker immediately and all at once.

Spinoza has consciously adopted the form of Euclid in the latter's *Elements*. How do the philosopher's definitions compare with those of the mathematician? The elements themselves, as presented in the definitions, appear to be self-evident (though this self-evidence can hardly be maintained retrospectively, especially of the twenty-third and final definition of Part I, the parallel definition; Euclid lists it as a definition and not as a postulate). However, there are no implied syllogisms, nor do they implicitly or explicitly address a history in which they or this likeness appear. Anselm's proof clearly does not have much at all in common with Spinoza's, and nothing like it can be found in Aquinas's five proofs. And Descartes's somewhat similar proof makes no reference to cause.

We may hear Spinoza in a way that honors both his Euclidean echoes and his uniqueness, by attending to the poetical thinking of his Greek forebears as subconsciously informing his notion of suprarational intuition. The definitions of the *Ethics* are themselves products of the third kind of knowledge. His arithmetical "illustration" can therefore serve to mislead if it is seen as a mere instance of more rapid rational calculation. Rather, it illustrates the unity and the instantaneity of the thought of the whole as determining the parts within it. It is the human activity of the mind that, in its own way, partakes of the whole of which it is a part. Its undertones are the Heraclitean logos, which is one and common; and the Parmenidean *estin*, the only true thought; even the Hesiodic precosmic poetic spectacle including the rape of Gē by Ouranos and the blood from it that gave rise to differentiated life and the division between the divine and the human.

Virtually to a person, scholars and readers of Spinoza affirm the remarkable "impersonality" of Spinoza's God, who loves no one and has no emotion. In this reinscription, Spinoza's suppression of eros in God, the abolition of struggle, of turmoil, of movement in divine existence, masks the very darkness out of which this marvelously bright surface is an image. In what sense do I call this surface *bright*, even marvelously bright? In terms of the sensible/intelligible distinction, there is nothing of sensation in it; in terms of the intellect, Spinoza appears to be thoroughly Cartesian insofar as nothing of sense or imagination is contained, only pure thought. However, such brightness can be not only conceived but also formulated in logos by virtue of the dark anteriot atmosphere that summons it.

Atmosphere

But this is to say that the marvelous brightness that makes itself manifest in Spinoza's *Ethics* as a Euclid-inspired discourse itself has the paramount character of an *atmosphere* as well. When one merely reads the words of various demonstrations and interprets them as decontextualized logical propositions and thus attempts to evaluate them in an unsuitable manner, the results can be disastrous. For example, in *The Rise of Scientific Philosophy*, a book so thoroughly stupid that it went through at least a score of printings, through the support of Anglo-American philosophers too careless and too arrogant to study their own history while mangling every significant figure in philosophy before him, Hans Reichenbach writes: "Spinoza needed the logical form as a backbone to support him in his suppression of emotions, in his uncommon indifference to the pleasures of passion. The Socratic intellectualization of ethics was thus used by him . . . for the construction of an ethics that disparages emotion. That is perhaps the most preposterous outcome of the ethico-cognitive parallelism."[41]

Here it is virtually impossible to find a proper beginning for comment. Might it be the condescending psychobabble? Or is it maybe that this author never read the many sections of the *Ethics* on the profound role of pleasures, especially the salubrious kinds? And Socratic intellectualization of ethics—while a certain (and relatively small) percentage of traditional Plato scholars held this view, it withers in the face of almost all of the dialogues, especially the *Phaedrus* and the *Symposium* but also the unfortunately neglected *Philebus* and large sections of the *Laws*.

However, Reichenbach's book can serve the positive function of exhibiting the sense of atmosphere that I here offer as well as illustrating the consequences of believing that things might be other than they are. He writes: "Had these mathematical developments [i.e., the putative proofs that geometry is basically an empirical science that approximates physical space] begun some two thousand years earlier, the history of philosophy would present a very different picture. In fact, one of Euclid's disciples might very well have been a Bolyai and might have discovered the non-Euclidean geometry. . . . Plato's doctrine of ideas would have been abandoned as lacking its basis in geometrical knowledge."[42]

Leaving aside this outrage to the already outrageous logical empiricism Reichenbach declares as the truth of philosophy, and doing so on occasion in comically plaintive terms,[43] such arbitrarily progressive and in principle reversible historicism calls forth what it cannot discern and would deny: that all thought occurs not only "within" but "in terms of" a surrounding ambience for which the German *Stimmung* might be a good descriptor.

Atmosphere: in Greek *atmos-* says "vapor," *sphaire* says globe or ball. An unseen yet palpable mixture of hot and cold, of wet and dry, recalling the thought of the presocratics, surrounds and gives human beings the climate within which we labor and within which we play. What can we say about this atmosphere? We still dwell within the atmosphere bequeathed by the Greeks. Even the benighted Reichenbach, as he struggles to pronounce a final verdict on all that came before him in terms of contemporary physics and geometry, works within that atmosphere.

One does not properly comment on an atmosphere or criticize some of the deeds accomplished within it. Such commentary and criticism presuppose the sway of the atmosphere. The series of arguments that seems to constitute the core of modern philosophy from Descartes, through Spinoza and Leibniz as well as through Locke, Berkeley, and Hume, to Kant are held within their sphere by a certain conception of reason that, as we have seen, has arisen neither ex nihilo nor outside a certain history. That history itself, including the very conception of history, is a function of the presupposed but concealed atmosphere.

In order to apprehend this atmosphere appropriately, it must be *breathed*. Hearing is one way Heraclitus speaks of attending to the common logos; *breathing* is another: "According to Heraclitus we become perceptive (*noeroi*) by drawing in this same divine logos (*theion logon*) by breathing it in (*anapnoēs*), and become forgetful when asleep, but we regain our *nous* when we awaken again . . . for in sleep, when the muscles of perception (*musantōn tōn aisthētokōn*) are closed, breathing is the only point of attachment to be preserved, like a kind of root . . . [and upon waking we meet] with its surroundings and put on its power of *logikēn*."[44] Regarding what we understand today as natural science, can we find witnesses to the atmosphere within which this "species" of activity takes place? We can; there are several.

In *Der Teil und das Ganze* (translated into English, quite oddly, as *Physics and Beyond*), Werner Heisenberg's conclusion seems to be that the whole is not physics but *philosophy*—Plato's thought especially. Throughout this work, in which Heisenberg presents a series of conversations, descriptions of wartime experiences from his youth, musical interludes, and his own evolving thoughts, the *Timaeus* emerges on several occasions and provokes ongoing disturbances in this scientist/philosopher's equilibrium. Initially in 1910, when he read the *Timaeus* as a teenager, he viewed the Platonic solids in what I will call a Reichenbachian manner: "The whole thing seemed to me to be wild speculation, pardonable on the ground that the Greeks lacked the necessary empirical knowledge."[45] He professed to read it repeatedly in order to exercise his proficiency in the Greek language, but found himself returning to it throughout his life. Even in his earliest, most skeptical readings he found himself "enthralled" by the notion that the smallest particles of matter must reduce to mathematical forms.

In his final chapter, which ends in 1965, his interpretation of Plato has both changed completely and has emphasized an aspect quite dissimilar in kind: "Whoever has meditated upon Plato's philosophy knows (*weiß*) that the world is *determined* through images (*daß die Welt durch Bilder bestimmt wird*)."[46] There are many alternatives to "determined" as a rendering of "bestimmt." *Stimmung* also has the sense of atmosphere, and of mood, and of tuning, or voice. *Bestimmen* can also mean "to destine," to designate, or "to prearrange." Thus, our habitual sense of *bestimmt* as "determined" can be heard as a echo of its prerational and mythical sense. In another place, Heisenberg strikingly locates the imagery required to think fundamental *energy* in "Heraclitean fire,"[47] of which Fragment 219 sounds: "Fire is exchange for all and all is exchange for fire just as gold is for things of use (*chrēmata*) and things of use are for gold."[48] This is another manner of thinking the one common logos, and with it comes a convincing indication that Heraclitus's logos cannot be rendered appropriately as "reason." There can be no doubt that Heisenberg breathes the atmosphere that grants him his being.

Der Teil und das Ganze also features a conversation that the author had with Einstein, in which the two towering physicists groped with the possible implications of Heisenberg's quantum theory, of which Einstein remained skeptical to the end. The discussion hinged on whether the simplicity of natural laws has an objective character or the subjective side could somehow limit such a claim. Read carefully, both thinkers held that the elements of nature were objective, and both affirmed a sui generis sense of wonder as they beheld this order. They agreed that the processes inside the atom could not be rendered in the usual language. But Einstein declared that Heisenberg's thought "is moving on very thin ice,"[49] for it concerns itself with what we know about nature rather than what nature does, which Einstein saw as the proper activity of science.

Einstein's Spinozism shines through this view. Two instances of it enable an interpretive recovery of its origin:

> Spinoza was the first to apply with strict consistency the idea of an all-pervasive determinism to human thought, feeling, and action. In my opinion, his point of view has not gained general acceptance by all those striving for clarity and logical rigor only because it requires

not only consistency of thought, but also unusual integrity, magnanimity, and—modesty.⁵⁰

It seems to me that the idea of a personal God is an anthropomorphic concept which I cannot take seriously. I feel also not able to imagine some will or goal outside the human sphere. My views are near to those of Spinoza: admiration for the beauty of and belief in the logical simplicity of the order and harmony which we can grasp humbly and only imperfectly. I believe that we have to content ourselves with our imperfect knowledge and understanding and treat values and moral obligations as a purely human problem—the most important of all human problems.⁵¹

Although this view of nature does not extend to what we call morals for Einstein as it does for Spinoza in the later parts of the *Ethics*, his "deterministic" view of nature includes components that recall Greek themes that underlie Spinoza's account of nature: "integrity" and "modesty" recall Socratic ignorance, as does "magnanimity" (*megalopsychia*), which also recalls not only Aristotle but also Heraclitus's *diēgeumai kata physin* (I describe in accord with nature).⁵² These three oddly balanced components occur in Proposition 11 and its proofs. This proposition reads: "God, or substance consisting of infinite attributes, each of which expresses eternal and infinite essence, necessarily exists."⁵³

Intuition and Infinitude

How must Proposition 11 be understood? Like the prior definitions, axioms, and propositions, Proposition 11 is known by intuition. The justifications for it—and for all future propositions in Part I—are themselves intuitions, that is, insights given immediately to the thinker. Here, the earlier illustration of the thinker who grasps a proportion all at once and the tradesman who multiplies the fractions in order to determine the missing number converge, albeit at a distance. One might look at it in this way: an infinite mind could grasp the whole in a single intuition. A finite mind—ours, the only one to which we have access—requires a chain of intuitions in order to grasp what it can of the whole. I dare to say that even the most sapient among us, the ones who can say *diēgeumai kata physin*, are themselves lumbering tradesmen when measured against the enormity of the task for thinking. Moving from intuition to intuition, Spinoza's human intuition reveals itself as *serial*. Here I speak of a temporality anterior to the time that is apprehended in the observation of moving bodies. It might be characterized as the temporality of the Heraclitean and Spinozist disclosure of the one logos, the "before and after" of the former and the ongoing derivations on the space of the pages of the latter that unfold "God or Nature."

To the "aristocratic tradesman," the thought of God or a substance with infinite attributes that one and all infinitely express God's essence immediately contains the thought of infinitely many attributes. However, what this tradesman must think and what she or he can access diverge within their ultimate unity. Thought and extension are the only two infinite attributes to which we have entry, each of which presents *what God is* fully. Spinoza's "abstract" notion of extension provides much material for thought. Its infinitude, which might seem to contravene our sense of quantity, nevertheless functions as the atmosphere within which any particular quantification draws it meaning. It recollects the Parmenidean *estin* in which before and after have no sense, and that strong Necessity binds.

Parmenides's ways of men, which are always backward turning, find their echo in Spinoza's response to philosophers who would deny extension to God on the grounds that infinite substance cannot be made up of finite parts. Indeed, it cannot—but finite parts do not together comprise infinite substance. Infinite substance cannot be measured at all from the side of particular quantity. Rather, infinite substance provides for the possibility of finite parts or, in my language here, the anterior atmospherics of substance allow for any finite measurement.

It may be proper to say that the Presocratics did not have a notion corresponding to our "infinite." However, Anaximander's *apeiron* does serve as a thought-provoking antecedent. It occurs in one Fragment, Fragment 119, as reported by Simplicius who is giving an account based on Theophrastus's discourses on earlier philosophy. Heidegger excludes *apeiron* from his commentary because it does not come from an accurately confirmed citation. However, there is good ground to hold this fragment as a faithful presentation of Anaximander; still further, there is good ground to comprehend the notion of an *apeiron* out of which all of the heavens and worlds come into being, as well as the coming into being and passing away of existing things.

Apeiron, considered grammatically, begins with a privative prefix: *a-peiron*. *Peras*, limit, seems to be the basis, which the privative prefix then somehow subtracts or denies, the way asymmetry points to the denial of symmetry, its basis. In an analogous manner, infinite begins with a privative prefix. However, for Spinoza "all determination is negation (*omnis determination est negatio*)" asserts absolute positivity of substance.[54] Infinitude means perfection, it means lacking *nothing*. The very notion of lack is radically alien to it. Every determination, in principle, lacks *something*, lacks what it is not. The thoroughgoing brightness, indicated earlier, in which nothing can be seen but only thought comes to the fore here. In order for something to be seen, a certain measure of darkness must surround it.

So how is the *thought* of infinitude possible? This is a question that resides at the edge of Spinoza's philosophy, both as its most intimate constituent and as the matter that most threatens this intimacy. Thought is, first and last, thought of infinitude. But thought also occurs only by virtue of an atmosphere. The atmosphere provides the ethos wherein such thought can occur, that is, it provides the play of light and dark that constitutes the place, the topos, of human dwelling.

Herein lies the ultimate source of the Spinozist contempt for final causes, even if he himself did not envision it in this manner. Final causes cannot occur within the atmospherics of human dwelling, but can only be "imagined" as outside it somehow—imagined in the thinnest second-order sense of being merely noncontradictory, just as Spinoza's "talking trees" are. Final causality outrages Spinozist logic, and also outrages Spinozist "ethics" in a narrower sense of the word. The home that Spinoza delineates, along with its anterior ancient Greek subterranean depth, is the only proper home for human beings.

Spinoza's *Symposium* and its Celebrated Antecedent

The entrance of Alcibiades in Plato's *Symposium* provides the missing component in the discussion of eros. Wine, flute music, earthboundness— these Dionysian characteristics that the "symposiasts" banished before the speeches began—return with the drunken and beautiful Alcibiades. Although no discernment is required in order to distinguish the discourses of Plato from those of Spinoza, one can nevertheless detect a kinship when this discernment pushes beyond its surface. In both Plato's express *Symposium* and Spinoza's implicit counterpart, all human apprehension occurs by virtue of bodies, just as all ideation occurs by virtue of thought.

The ascent recounted in Diotima's speech to Socrates affirms that the first step on the ladder consists of the eros of one beautiful body (begetting beautiful logoi), and moves up to the next step that consists of the eros of all beautiful bodies. The beauty of souls constitutes the next level followed by the eros of customs and daily practices. The ultimate step and the goal toward which its predecessors aimed is the eros of beauty itself—disembodied, unsullied, pure, absolute. As I have insisted elsewhere,[55] this ascent fills out only one side of the symposium, the Apollonian side. The entrance of Alcibiades completes the symposium by providing the Dionysian side. Only then does the symposium become a true *sum-posion*, a drinking of wine together.

In order to grasp the kinship between Plato's *Symposium* and Spinoza's implicit counterpart, Gilles Deleuze's often-revealing takes on the great thinkers of the past are especially illuminating in his reflections on Spinoza.[56] In one sense, Deleuze insightfully imagines a particular human being—himself, Spinoza—walking about and encountering other people. It is understood that the people are, in the Cartesian parlance, extended things. However, the peripatetic Spinozist always finds himself in the midst of ever-changing ideas. Deleuze calls these ongoing changes "variations." However, as the term *idea* indicates, these bodies cannot merely be bodies. Rather, the human being on the street in motion always moves from one degree of perfection to another.

The examples he employs are far-reaching. On the street, Deleuze encounters a disagreeable Pierre and a pleasant Paul soon afterward. The former, the idea of Pierre, contains a smaller degree of perfection than the idea of Paul. We might imagine, for the sake of the citation below, a displeasing Joop and a pleasing Joos, or a displeasing Geertje and a pleasing Gerdi:

> I would say that, to the extent that ideas succeed each other in us, each one having its own degree of perfection, its degree of reality or intrinsic perfection, the one who has these ideas, in this case me, never stops passing from one degree of perfection to another. In other words there is a continuous variation in the form of an increase-diminution-increase-diminution of the power of acting or the force of existing of someone according to the ideas that s/he has. *Feel how beauty shines through this difficult exercise.* This representation of existence already isn't bad, it really is existence in the street, it's necessary to imagine Spinoza strolling about, and he truly lives existence as this kind of continuous variation: to the extent that an idea replaces another, I never cease to pass from one degree of perfection to another, however miniscule the difference, *and this kind of melodic*

line of continuous variation will define affect (*affectus*) in its correlation with ideas and at the same time in its difference in nature from ideas. We account for this difference in nature and this correlation.[57]

As in his early book on Hume,[58] Deleuze shows himself to be one of the very few who can think along with his extraordinary forebears. The results of these thoughts are manifold. Concerning Spinoza's implicit symposium, Deleuze senses the concealed undertones that essentially belong to it. First and foremost, the ascent to ideas takes its departure from movements of the body. But where, one might ask, is eros, love in the discourse? And indeed, what is love for Spinoza? Is it allied with honor, as in Phaedrus's speech in Plato's *Symposium*? With custom and law, as in Pausanias's? With harmony, as in Eryximachus's? With halved beings seeking and finding their severed other halves, as in Aristophanes's? With youth and beauty, as in Agathon's? Is it a *daimon*, mediating between gods and humans for the sake of birth in beauty, as in Socrates's? Can it somehow be sighted in a rare person like Socrates, as Alcibiades might think? Spinoza: none of the above, indeed nothing resembling any of the above: "Love is pleasure accompanied by the idea of an external cause."[59]

While it is surely a reach to read the Platonic discourses on eros into Spinoza's text, I will hazard this reach. In Deleuze's stimulating and especially perceptive response to Spinoza's thought, we find the way up from bodies to ideas, from wandering in the street experiencing the increase-diminution-increase-diminution of the power of acting or the force of existing as the human being encounters various entities to reflecting upon the degrees of perfection in their corresponding ideas, to imaging the ascent from bodies to *eidê* in a unified sweep. Beauty enters the Spinozist discourse in precisely the manner that Deleuze marks: (1) in the feeling of beauty that shines through the difficult account; and (2) the melodic line of continuous variation will define affect (*affectus*) in its correlation with ideas and at the same time in its difference in nature from ideas. Virtually alone among commentators, fellow thinker Deleuze hears the music that animates Spinoza's discourse. He is no mere scholar, but a member of Schopenhauer's Republic of Geniuses who speak to one another across generations.

Spinoza's Alcibiades can be located in the striking treatment of the emotions. There is no drunkenly anguished account along the lines of

Alcibiades's grandiloquence on his love/hatred of Socrates. Rather, his words accord with the language in which the *Ethics* is cast: "Therefore, I shall treat of the nature and power of the affects, and the power of the mind over them, by the same method by which, in the preceding parts, I treated God and the mind, I have used in treating of God and the mind, and I shall consider human actions and appetites just as if it were an investigation into lines, planes, or bodies."[60]

Since Spinoza defined love as pleasure accompanied by the idea of an external cause, the definition of hatred is easily extrapolated: hatred is pain accompanied by the idea of an external cause. As in the tortured soul of Alcibiades but recast in the language of Spinozist *Ethics*, love and hate find themselves frequently interacting. Desire is "man's very essence, insofar as it is conceived to be determined, from any given affection of it, to do something."[61] While hatred constitutes one pole of desire, love constitutes the other. Once the recognition that love and hate intertwine in Spinoza, the undertow of the ancient archaic pull becomes apparent. I shall cite several salient "Ethical" propositions:

> P20: He who imagines that what he hates will be destroyed will rejoice.[62]
>
> P22: If we imagine that someone to affect with joy a thing that we love, we shall be affected with love toward him. If, on the other hand, we imagine him to affect the same thing with sadness, we shall also be affected with hate toward him.[63]
>
> P23: He who imagines that what he hates to be affected with sadness will rejoice; if, on the other hand, he should imagine it to be affected with joy, he will be saddened.[64]
>
> P24: If we imagine someone to affect with joy a thing we hate, we shall be affected with hate toward him also. On the other hand, if we imagine him to affect the same thing with sadness, we shall be affected with love toward him.[65]

Spinoza's famous "intellectual love of God," then, results in freedom from pain and accordingly from hatred as well. This explains his declaration: "It should be noted that sickness of the mind and misfortunes take their origins especially from too much love toward a thing which is liable to many variations and which we can never really possess. For no one is disturbed or anxious concerning anything unless he loves it, nor do wrongs, suspicions, and enmities arise except from love of a thing which no one can really fully possess."⁶⁶ Such orientation toward "unstable" things enmeshes one within the cycle of love and hatred indicated by the three propositions cited above.

Even more provocatively, "P31: If we imagine that someone loves, desires, or hates something that we ourselves love, desire, or hate, we shall thereby love, desire, or hate it with greater constancy. But if we imagine that he is averse to what we love, or the opposite..., then we shall undergo a vacillation of mind."⁶⁷

The language is far from Hesiod's, but the notion of unnerving the limbs and overcoming sense can certainly be heard beneath the so-called rational language that conceals the anterior subsoil. Listen also to the following from Heraclitus: "Disease makes health pleasant and good, hunger satiety, weariness rest (*Nousos hugeiēn epoiēsen hēdu kai agathon, limos koron, kamatos anapausin*)."⁶⁸ Opposition inscribes itself into the life of mortals. In Spinoza, it does so as love/hatred.

Plato's *Symposium* does not consist of logoi on hatred. This is a major difference from the Platonic dialogue, and the attention given to this latter phenomenon, apart from which the phenomenon of love cannot be conceived, provides access to the tremoring Greek substratum. One need not look far into Greek poetry to locate this phenomenon.

The hatred of Aias for Odysseus comes to mind, which issued from the contest for Achilles's armor. The language of reason may seem inadequate when measured against, for example, the language of Sophocles in *Aias*:

> ATHENA: I'll tell you this: Ajax did those killings, as you suspected.
>
> ODYSSEUS: Why would he do that? [40] Why turn his hands to such a senseless act?
>
> ATHENA: The weapons—that armour from Achilles—it made him insanely angry.   50
>
> ODYSSEUS: But then why would he slaughter all the animals?
>
> ATHENA: He thought he was staining both his hands with blood from you.
>
> ODYSSEUS: You mean this was his plan against the Argives?
>
> ATHENA: Yes—and it would have worked, if I had not been paying attention.
>
> ODYSSEUS: How could he have done something so reckless? How could his mind have been so rash?

ATHENA: At night in secret he crept out alone after you.

ODYSSEUS: How close was he? Did he get to his target?   60

ATHENA: He reached the camp of both commanders—he made it right up to their double gates.

ODYSSEUS: If he was so insanely keen for slaughter, [50] how could he prevent his hands from killing?

ATHENA: I stopped him. I threw down into his eyes an overwhelming sense of murderous joy . . . be brave. Do not back off or look upon this man as any threat to you. I will avert his eyes, so he will never see your face. *[Calling to Ajax inside the hut]*

You in there—   90

the one who's tying up his prisoner's arms—I'm calling you! I'm shouting now for Ajax! Come on out here! Outside the hut! In front!

ODYSSEUS: Athena! What are you doing? Don't call him! Don't bring him out here!

ATHENA: Just be patient. Don't run the risk of being called a coward.

Spinoza writes much more prosaically that such disturbances of mind arise from love toward a thing that one can never completely possess. Not only does the shield of Achilles belong among such things, but so too do votes of the council members who were persuaded to award the arms to Odysseus by the latter's superior rhetoric and the honor represented by the arms and the sentiment of the council. Unlike most analyses, I believe that Aias's hatred of Athena seems to have considerable justification: he is the only Hellenic warrior who did not receive divine aid. When Athena offered her assistance to Aias during the Trojan War, he offended her merely by refusing her offer: and directing her to help someone else, "for where I bide, no enemy will break through."[69]

What about the Greek gods and goddesses in this context? They bear no resemblance whatsoever to Spinoza's "God, or Nature," nor are they "supernatural" beings. If one were to attempt to characterize them in Spinozist terms, they are beings that act in accord with their own nature, displaying will analogues that are no freer than their human counterparts. In this sense, they present what Nietzsche said in *The Birth of Tragedy*, Section 3: "In this way, the gods justify the lives of men, because they themselves live it—that is the only satisfactory theodicy!"[70]

From that human point of view that Spinoza is at pains to reject, Athena grows angry at Aias for the latter's hubristic refusal of her generous offer and punishes him by protecting his sworn enemy Odysseus as she humiliates the noble Aias. However, a Spinozist reading yields no moral lesson at all; what happened at Troy and afterward could not have occurred in any other way. God, too, is bound by necessity, and the wise human being loves God.

The sweep of the *Symposium* demonstrates that the image of Socrates has incorporated both the Apollonian and the Dionysian, both the impulse toward the more divine measure of order and self-knowledge with the impulse toward the more earthbound measure of truth disclosed through wine. To make a brief taxonomic observation, Socrates *serves* Apollo in the city; he is not Apollo nor is he "Apollonian" himself. His strangeness consists in the rare quality of his humanity, not in the slightest resemblance to any divinity however the latter might be imagined. In Spinoza's language, Socrates provokes not only wonder (*admiratio*), which arises from the strangeness of a thing, but devotion, which results when wonder is accompanied by the circumstance that the person wondered at possesses more virtue than we do.[71]

Hoi Polloi

The division between the common people, the many, and those few whose status elevates them above their more ordinary counterparts, occurs now and again in philosophy as it does in many areas of life and in many ways. Such divisions are often drawn in terms of birth, income, and political power. In philosophy, however, the diffrentiation takes place in accorddance with principled insight as distinguished from haphazardness judgment.

"The mob is fearsome, if it does not fear. So it is not surprising that the prophets have been so zealous in commending humility, repentance, and reverence."[72] "The mob," aka *hoi polloi*, plays a consequential role in ancient thought. As we have seen, Herclitus delineates the common logos in distinction from *hoi polloi* who suppose that they have their own insight. Indeed, we do not speak of two strata of human beings, *hoi aristoi* and *hoi polloi*: membership in the latter comes automatically with the belief that one has one's own insight. For Parmenides, the ways of mortals for whom *estin* is not the way, and who instead follow appearance, are foolish, backward-turning. However, in this matter the echoes of the Platonic dialogues sound clearest and most emphatic.

This thought, develops further with Socrates of the *Crito*. There, the eponymous interlocutor argues that one must care about the judgment of *hoi polloi*—Socrates's death sentence proves that *hoi polloi* can do the greatest harm if one is slandered among them. The reply: "It would be useful (*ōphelon*) if *hoi polloi* could do the greatest harm, for then they could do the greatest good, which would be beautiful—but now, they can do neither. They cannot make someone either wise or foolish, since they inflict things haphazardly (*tuchosi*)" (44d).

To Crito's accusation that Socrates is neglecting matters concerning money, reputation, and familial obligations by his refusal to escape, the reply is that such considerations belong not to those who value justice but to *hoi polloi*, who easily put people to death and would bring them to life again without any thought if they could. Ultimately, *hoi polloi* is a normative rather than a merely descriptive characterization, which indicates arbitrary judgment rather than judgment guided by the best logos. Socrates models the latter by speaking in the voice of the laws from which he draws the most convincing conclusion, namely, that he would perpetrate malignant injustice by escaping from Athens, which has given him so much of value.

Consider also the passage in *Republic* VI, where Socrates describes the stance of the philosopher amid *hoi polloi* of the city, whom he likens to "a human being who has fallen in with wild beasts and is neither willing to join them in doing injustice or sufficient as one man to resist all the savage animals." This is the most scathing characterization of *hoi polloi*, and the most negative view of the philosopher's plight among his fellow men and women.

> Seeing others filled with lawlessness, he is content (*agapa*) if somehow he can live his life here pure of injustice and unholy deeds, and take his leave from it graciously and cheerfully with fair hope.
> "Well," [Adeimantus] said, "he would leave having accomplished not the least of things."
> But not the greatest either, I said, if he didn't chance upon a suitable regime. For in a suitable one he himself would grow more and save the common things along with the private. (496d–497a)

Spinoza's modern *Ethics* concludes conspicuously with the words, "All excellent things are as difficult as they are rare."[73] While his complex views of democracy ascribe many surprisingly favorable qualities to it (as well as some that we would surely reject today), his philosophical view of "men"—aka the many, *hoi polloi*—bears a close resemblance to those articulated by Socrates in the Platonic dialogues. For example, he ridicules those who believe that nature acts for an end by virtue of final causes. "But while they sought to show that Nature does nothing in vain (i.e., nothing not of use to men), they seem to have shown only that Nature and the gods are as mad as men."[74] In other words, they mistake figments of their imagination (*entia imaginationes*) for things of reason (*entia rationis*).[75]

> So all arguments drawn from such notions against me can be easily refuted. For many are wont to argue on the following lines: If everything has followed from the necessity of God's most perfect nature, why does Nature display so many imperfections, such as rottenness to the point of putridity, nauseating ugliness, confusion, evil, sin, and so on? But . . . these are easily refuted. For the perfection of things should be measured solely from their own nature and power; nor are things more or less perfect to the extent that they please or offend human senses, serve or oppose human interests.[76]

He also expresses contempt for humility and repentance, as these do not arise from reason but rather from the contemplation of weakness. However, he does not go so far as to condemn them completely. He merely declares that they are not virtues. Humility and repentance may lead to virtue insofar as these put human beings in touch with their essence, which may subsequently be raised to knowledge that things could not occur otherwise than they have. Spinoza offers some praise to the prophets who counseled humility and repentance despite their not being virtues. His reasoning is the following: "For if men of weak spirit should equally be subject to pride, and should be ashamed of nothing and afraid of nothing, by what bonds could they be held together and bound?"

The contemporary philosophical Zeitgeist abhors such condescension, even as it belies the liberal side of Spinoza's political views, which champion both the natural equality of men and the need for collective deliberations. However, contempt for *hoi polloi* and respect for human nature hardly contradict one another. No human being is consigned to *hoi polloi* by way of birth or upbringing. Spinoza himself did not live a socially aristocratic life. He earned his keep by giving private lessons, and as a lens grinder of uncommon talent. However, one cannot deny his awareness of his own high worthiness.

Socrates also affirmed that persuasion of his fellow citizens belong to the responsibilities of the philosopher. He ascribed the reason for the hostility of *hoi polloi* to philosophy to the viciousness and "queerness" (487d) of those who have arrogated its name but do not belong, and would explain gently, not harshly, that those who deserve the name have been driven to a kind of internal exile by those who do not belong. Just as Spinoza praised the prophets for counseling humility and repentance both to calm *hoi polloi* and to make it possible for some to "lead the life of the blessed," likewise, Socrates in the *Republic* holds that although *hoi polloi* cannot be philosophical, some can be persuaded toward love of learning if spoken to soothingly and properly (499e–500a). Spinoza also directs the sapient human being to speak softly and respectfully to the majority, both to keep its behavior from becoming dangerously unruly and to lead it toward a life governed by reason to a greater degree.

All of the above bespeaks the presence of a portrait of Socrates inscribed into Spinoza's *Ethics*. This portrait receives still greater distinctness when their discourses on death are considered. Socrates—the image of Socrates—serves as Spinoza's singular anteriority.

Death

Spinoza writes, "A free man thinks of death least of all things, and his wisdom is a meditation of life, not of death."[77] How this claim reconciles with the claim in Plato's *Phaedo* requires another address toward what lies beneath.[78] On his final day, as recorded by Phaedo, Socrates characterizes philosophy in the following manner:

> "And now I will make answer to you, O my judges, and show that he who has lived as a true philosopher has reason to be of good cheer when he is about to die, and that after death he may hope to receive the greatest good in the other world. And how this may be, Simmias and Cebes, I will endeavor to explain. For I deem that the true disciple of philosophy is likely to be misunderstood by other men; they do not perceive that he is ever pursuing death and dying; and if this is true, why, having had the desire of death all his life long, should he repine at the arrival of that which he has been always pursuing and desiring?"
>
> "And Simmias laughed." (63e–64a)

Philosophy as practicing dying, as regarding death as philosophy's aim—what does this mean? It remains one of the most provocative passages in the history of philosophy, as well as one of the most frequently pondered. The Platonic text has Socrates presenting its meaning as the separation of the soul from the body, with the at least implicit consequence that, freed from its imprisonment therein, it can experience its ideas purified from admixture. However, this notion of philosophy cannot be found in any of the other (presumably later) dialogues. In this remark on philosophy, Socrates functions here as Apollo's oracle.

What is death, if indeed there is any sense in referring to death as if calling it a "what" is at all appropriate? Death is always present in its absence. For both Socrates and Spinoza, death—which lies at once beneath and beyond—presents itself as anteriority par excellence. The definition of being free in the *Ethics*, Definition 7, reads: "That thing is said to be free [*liber*] which exists solely from the necessity of its own nature. . . . A thing is said to be necessary [*necessarius*] or rather, constrained [*coactus*], if it is determined by another thing to exist and to act in a definite and determinate way."[79]

Accordingly, there can be only one free being. However, insofar as there remains the possibility of intellectual love of God, a human being may have a share in God's freedom—by accepting the necessity according to which all things unfold and belong. The anathema to which Spinoza found himself subject rested largely on his denial of the immortality of the soul, a matter that seems almost quaint in our day. He did maintain that the eternal aspect of the mind remained after the body expired, but this did not at all entail temporal life or consciousness. Although his argument caused and causes some controversy, the conclusion follows straightforwardly from earlier parts of the *Ethics*. To those of us who might look for some comfort à la W. C. Fields looking for loopholes in the Bible on his deathbed, we find none.

How does the above stand with philosophy as practicing dying? First of all, the crucial passage in the *Phaedo* states that the greatest of evils consists in the soul's complicity (the Greek is *xullêptor*) in its own imprisonment. There seem to be incontrovertible passages that advocate the desirability of the soul's separation from the body. However, these passages can certainly be understood as belonging to the context of the dialogue between Simmias and Cebes, both of whom fear death and seek solace from Socrates. The complicity of the soul constitutes the reason for its fear of death. Without this complicity, fear departs: "'In fact, Simmias,' he said, 'those who philosophize rightly make dying their care, and *of human beings to them least of all is being dead terrifying*.... Then will the man who's genuinely in love with thoughtfulness and has taken a firm hold of this hope that nowhere else but in Hades would he encounter it in a manner worth speaking of'" (67A-68B; emphasis added).

If the two texts are placed beside one another, their differences are particularly apparent. But if the Platonic texts are heard to sound the undercurrents of Spinoza's, then their interrelation abides as the subterrestrial aspect occurring in dissonant concert with the eternal aspect.

There are also two accounts of deportment toward death in the *Apology*. According to the first, it is disgraceful to fear death since one is altogether ignorant concerning the nature of its occurrence (29a-b). According to the second, which occurs in a mythical context—that is, one dictated by the *daimonion* near the *Apology*'s end—death is a good. Death will consist either of a permanently uninterrupted sleep or of relocation to Hades, where Socrates can question the gods and heroes and true judges, testing one and all as he has done on earth in order to determine whether they are wise or not (40c-41c). In both cases, fear never materializes.

The argument that it is disgraceful to fear death on account of our ignorance concerning it is accompanied by a replacement: we should fear doing injustice since we know that doing injustice is evil. This unfolds into the advice Socrates gives to his would-be acquitters that it is *necessary (dei)* to be cheerful in the face of death, to believe that the gods are mindful of the affairs of human beings, and that to a good human being no harm can come either in life or thereafter (41c-d). Clearly, "harm" consists in "doing injustice"; this way is open to human choice. Being accused unjustly and even being put to death as a result of such false accusations are not. These concerns are audible in Spinoza's characterization of what he calls "external causes": "human power is very limited and is infinitely surpassed by the power of external causes, so we do not have absolute power to adapt to our purposes things external to us. However, we shall patiently bear whatever happens to us that is required by consideration to our own advantage, if we are conscious that we have done our duty and that our power was not extensive enough to have avoided the said things, and that we are part of the whole of Nature whose order we follow."[80]

If there is a decisive parallel between Socrates of the dialogues and Spinoza, the property of cheerfulness joins them, and marks them as philosophers of a temperament. P43 of the *Ethics* says: "Cheerfulness cannot be excessive, it is always good. On the other hand, melancholy is always bad.[81]" The cheerfulness of Socrates marks his bearing in every dialogue in which he appears. Even in the *Apology*, where he seems to speak to his jury with an uncommon degree of harshness, his final words commend cheerfulness to himself and to those who voted for his acquittal. As in the case of his modern monotheistic reborn embodiment, philosophy is co-extensive with the greatest delight available for a human being.

For better or for worse (I say "for worse'), this attitude finds itself in only a small minority. As Continental philosophy has become more focused on specifically political themes, for example, feminism, critical race theory, postcolonial theory, and queer theory, the seriousness of these issues to their champions can and sometimes does make cheerfulness seem frivolous. Nevertheless, I claim that cheerfulness marks those among philosophy's great figures who have determined the scope and the boundaries of our discipline,[82] and implicitly informs the many proposals for redress of injustice.[83]

Together with the inscribed image of Socrates spoken of above, I am persuaded of the appropriateness of reading the life of Spinoza together with the life of Socrates. From accounts that are considered reliable, Spinoza's conduct has to be regarded as virtually blameless, even saintly. In the face of excommunication from the Jewish faith into which he was born, his bearing did not change and there is no evidence of any grudge toward those religious "authorities" who cursed him and banished him in the most ringing and acrimonious terms.[84] His alleged solitariness turns out not to be true: he had many friends in Amsterdam and Rotterdam just as Socrates had many friends in Athens with whom he could discuss philosophical matters.

However, we must be content with the *image* of Spinoza, just as we must be with the image of Socrates. What does Spinoza's *Ethics* reveal about images and imaginations? I must answer: very little, and very much. Doctrinally speaking, imagination belongs to the lowest kind of knowledge. Knowledge of the first kind, as we have seen, is called "*opinion, or imagination*."[85] Of the three kinds, only the latter knowledge can be false. Imagination cannot be regarded as true or false in itself; the idea that it imagines is true insofar as it conforms to the thing of which it is the idea, and false insofar as the idea does not so conform. Spinoza separates it decisively from the intellect—imagination (and memory) only pertains to the ever-changing bodily element of human life. When the body dies, the intellect possesses a certain timeless and nonconscious immortality unlike any religiously proposed and depicted afterlife. Imagination belongs to the finite element of the human being.

However, Spinoza casts his *Ethics* in the express image of Euclid's *Elements*. His definitions, axioms, and propositions image those of Euclid; even if one were to reverse the order, one would be compelled to say that in order of significance, Euclid's proofs image the ontology of Spinoza. Finally, just as Hesiod imagined his poem *Theogony*, we should also say that Spinoza imagined his *Ethics*. In the latter, imagination is more fully present the more it is suppressed in the discourse. The Muses inspired Hesiod—in our language a nonrational source that bestows great benefits on the human race. Who or what inspired Spinoza? Euclid? Descartes? Or is it the same sensed awareness of the abyssal originary withdrawal that animated the Greeks?

I have advanced the view that the "impersonality" of God, who loves no one and has no emotion, is Spinoza's inscribed suppression of the Greek eros. Struggle, turmoil, play, and generally movement (becoming) in divine existence mask the very darkness out of which this marvelously bright surface is an image. It is time for a reinscription of eros in what for Spinoza is a region of pure intelligibility. Such a reinscription cannot but disturb this irenic picture according to which the enjoyment of blessedness consists in the total control over our lusts. Even this view draws from an atmosphere to which darkness essentially belongs, and which remains haunted by the very shadows it would banish.

Spinoza's rationalism cannot be praised highly enough. The clarity of his reasoning and the insistence of his intellectualism carry within them the hidden depths driving modern philosophy. In this unique way, his discourse surpasses the discourses of his colleagues both on the Continent and in England during that great period. The bugaboo of final cause has been decisively removed from the superabundance of problematic philosophical issues. The nature of the origin of our ideas has also been taken away from the list, as have the vexing matters connected with particularity and universality. Spinoza is modern philosophy *purified*.

76 | A Dark History of Modern Philosophy

The rewriting of the history of modern philosophy thus takes its departure from his thought.

Notes

1. Heraclitus, *The Presocratic Philosophers*, ed. G. S. Kirk, J. E. Raven, and M. Schofield (Cambridge: Cambridge University Press, 1983), Frag. 247, 210–211. All future references to this book shall begin with the name of the philosopher cited, followed by "in Kirk et al., *Presocratic Philosophers*," the fragment number listed in the text, and the page number of the text on which the fragment is found. I will retranslate many of the fragments.

2. Martin Heidegger, *Gesamtausgabe*, Band 9 (Frankfurt am Main: Vittorio Klostermann, 1975), 354, 185.

3. For example, Pluto, Orkus.

4. Greek is in another form: *daimona*.

5. Plato, *The Republic of Plato*, trans. Allan Bloom (New York: Basic Books, 1968), 617e.

6. John Sallis, *On Translation* (Bloomington: Indiana University Press), 6.

7. Heraclitus, in Kirk et al., *Presocratic Philosophers*, Frag. 204, 108.

8. René Descartes, *Discourse on Method and Meditations on First Philosophy*, 4th ed., trans. Donald Cress (Indianapolis: Hackett, 1998), 1.

9. Heraclitus, in Kirk et al., *Presocratic Philosophers*, Frag. 196, 187.

10. Benedictus de Spinoza, *The Ethics*, in *A Spinoza Reader: The Ethics and Other Works*, ed. and trans. Edwin Curley (Princeton, NJ: Princeton University Press, 1994), II, D2, 115–116.

11. Parmenides, in Kirk et al., *Presocratic Philosophers*, Frag. 295, 248.

12. Martin Heidegger, *An Introduction to Metaphysics*, trans. Ralph Mannheim (Garden City, NY: Doubleday Anchor, 1961), 115.

13. Ibid., 121.

14. Spinoza, *Ethics*, I, P16, 97.

15. Ibid., I, D7, 86.

16. Ibid., I, P29, 104.

17. Descartes, *Discourse on Method*, Cor. 1, 59.

18. Spinoza, *Ethics*, I, P32, 105.

19. Immanuel Kant, *Critique of Practical Reason*, trans. Lewis White Beck (Indianapolis: Bobbs-Merrill, 1956), 10 (Akad. 10).

20. Spinoza, *Ethics*, Part IV, P 8, 204.

21. In the final section, on Nietzsche, I will take up the theme of tragedy—and the cheerfulness that is proper to its reception.

22. Parmenides, in Kirk et al., *Presocratic Philosophers*, Frag. 293, 247.

23. Ibid., Frag. 24, 247.

24. See Martin Heidegger, *What Is Called Thinking?*, trans. J. Glenn Gray (New York: Harper Torchbooks, 1972), Part 2, esp. 250–251.

25. Henry G. Liddell and Robert Scott, *An Intermediate Greek–English Lexicon: Founded upon Liddell and Scott's Greek English Lexicon* (Oxford: Oxford University Press, 1975), 533–534.
26. Parmenides, in Kirk et al., *Presocratic Philosophers*, Frag. 298, 251.
27. Ibid., Frag. 300, 254.
28. Spinoza, *Ethics*, 85.
29. Ibid.
30. Ibid.
31. Ibid.
32. Ibid.
33. *Huperēphanos* could also mean "arrogant," or "grandiose." It carries the sense of excess (*huper-*), and the word is used with a feeling of self-deprecating playfulness.
34. Aristotle, *Physics* 3/II, 194b18–195a3, cited in *The Basic Works of Aristotle*, trans. Richard McKeon (New York: Modern Library Reissue, 2009).
35. Thomas Aquinas, *The Summa Theologica*, trans. Anton C. Pegis (New York: Modern Library, 1948), 45–46.
36. Spinoza, *Ethics*, 89.
37. Parmenides, in Kirk et al., *Presocratic Philosophers*, Frag. 293 (*palintropos*), 247.
38. John Sallis, *Force of Imagination: The Sense of the Elemental* (Bloomington: Indiana University Press, 2000), 87.
39. Descartes, *Discourse on Method*, 1.
40. Spinoza, *Ethics*, P40, Sch 2, IV, 141.
41. Hans Reichenbach, *The Rise of Scientific Philosophy* (Berkeley: University of California Press, 1968), 55.
42. Ibid., 142.
43. "But truth is a powerful weapon, and it has at all times collected followers among the best. There is good evidence that that the circle of its followers is growing larger and larger. And that is all that can be hoped for." Ibid., 143.
44. Heraclitus, in Kirk et al., *Presocratic Philosophers*, Frag. 234, 205. I have changed part of their translation.
45. Werner Heisenberg, *Physics and Beyond: Encounters and Conversations* (New York: Harper Torchbooks, 1972), 8.
46. Ibid., 246. Emphasis added.
47. Werner Heisenberg, "Heisenberg: 'Grundlegende Voraussetzungen,'" cited in Martin Heidegger, *Martin Heidegger zum siebzigsten Geburtstag; Festschrift* (Pfullingen: Günther Neske 1959), 291–297. Heisenberg's essay was part of a *Festschrift* dedicated to Martin Heidegger on his 70th birthday. Many other noted figures also contributed.
48. Heraclitus, in Kirk et al., *Presocratic Philosophers*, Frag. 219, 197–198.
49. Heisenberg, *Physics and Beyond*, 68. The German reads literally "in a dangerous direction" (Der Teil und das Ganze) (Munich: dtv, 1969), 85.
50. Letter to Dagobert Runes, September 8, 1932, Einstein Archive, reel 33-286, cited in Max Jammer, *Einstein and Religion* (Princeton, NJ: Princeton University Press, 1999), 44–45.

51. Letter to Murray W. Gross, April 26, 1947, Einstein Archive, reel 33-324, cited in Jammer, *Einstein and Religion*, 138–139.
52. Heraclitus, in Kirk et al., *Presocratic Philosophers*, Frag. 194, 186–187.
53. Spinoza, *Ethics*, P11, 91.
54. Letter to Jarig Jellis, June 2, 1674, cited in Spinoza, *Spinoza Reader*.
55. Bernard Freydberg, *The Play of the Platonic Dialogues* (New York: Peter Lang, 1997), 58–61.
56. Bernard Freydberg, *David Hume: Platonic Philosopher, Continental Ancestor* (Albany: State University of New York Press, 2012), 9–15.
57. Gilles Deleuze, "On Spinoza," Lectures by Gilles Deleuze (blog), February 2007, http://deleuzelectures.blogspot.com/2007/02/on-spinoza.html. Emphasis added.
58. Gilles Deleuze, *Empiricism and Subjectivity: An Essay on Hume's Theory of Human Nature* (New York: Columbia University Press, 2001).
59. Spinoza, *Ethics*, Part III, 94.
60. Ibid., Preface to Part III, 153.
61. Ibid., Part III, 188.
62. Ibid., Part III, 165.
63. Ibid., Part III, 166.
64. Ibid.
65. Ibid., Part III, 167.
66. Ibid., Part V, 152.
67. Ibid., Part III, 77.
68. Heraclitus, in Kirk et al., *Presocratic Philosophers*, Frag. 201, 188.
69. Sophocles, *Ajax*, in *Sophocles Vol. I*, trans. Hugh Lloyd-Jones (Cambridge MA: Harvard University Press, 1997), 772.
70. Friedrich Nietzsche, *The Birth of Tragedy and The Case of Wagner*, trans. Walter Kaufmann (New York: Vintage, 1967), 43.
71. Spinoza, *Ethics*, Part III, P52, 87, Definitions of Emotions, 95.
72. Ibid., Part IV, 129. Emphasis added.
73. Ibid., Part V, 161.
74. Ibid., Part I, Appendix, 110.
75. Ibid., part I, Appendix, 114–115.
76. Spinoza, Project Gutenberg Ebook of the *Ethics*. Last updated July 2007. This passage comes from a different edition of the Curley translation.
77. Spinoza, *Ethics,*, Part IV, 135.
78. Ibid., 135, Part IV, P67.
79. Ibid, Part I, 86.
80. Ibid., Part IV, 142.
81. Ibid., Part IV, 124.
82. Letter 79 of Johann Gottfried Herder, "Letters on the Advancement of Humanity" in *Another Philosophy of History and Selected Political Writings*, trans. Ioannis Evrigenis and Daniel Pellerin (Indianapolis: Hackett, 2004).
83. Kant's moral law, for example, undergirds every just liberation movement. The principle of humanity, which commands that humans (ourselves included) be

treated as ends and not merely as means, is at least tacitly presupposed in such movements.

84. A small sample follows: "cursed be he by day, and cursed be he by night; cursed be he when he lieth down, and cursed be he when he riseth up; cursed be he when he goeth out, and cursed be he when he cometh in; the Lord will not pardon him." This to one of the best and gentlest of human beings.

85. Spinoza, *Ethics*, Part II, P40, Sch 2, 51.

Intermezzo

On the Putative History of German Idealism

> Hegel, whose rationalism one cannot sufficiently praise and vilify (*schmähen*).
>
> Martin Heidegger

WHAT MAKES HEGEL'S rationalism stand beyond sufficient praise? In his *Phenomenology of Spirit*, every shape of consciousness shows itself as a shape of reason in the process of becoming. More precisely, unconscious reason—Being in and for itself in itself—gradually becomes self-conscious, that is, being in and for itself in and for itself.

The *Science of Logic* presupposes the *Phenomenology*. In it, liberated self- conscious reason thinks pure Being *schlechthin* as beginning the *Logic*. No one else has done so. Logic for Hegel is "truth without veil and in its own absolute nature. It can further be said that it is the presentation of God as he is in his eternal essence before (*vor*) the creation of nature and of a finite mind."[1] The "vor" clearly speaks to an ontological rather than a temporal priority. All thought derives from Being, beginning with the "Nothing" into which Being unfolds on account of its pure emptiness and into the unity of Being and Nothing as "Becoming."

Thought has its own proper milieu for Hegel, though he acknowledges that it is difficult to locate "space for a passionless calm that is only left open to thinking knowledge (*der nur zur denkenden Erkenntnis*)."[2] One can certainly hear Spinozist echoes that account for Hegel's remark that all who philosophize are Spinozists at first. For Hegel, one cannot remain with Spinozism on account of its solely negative notion of determination. However, Spinoza remains as what Hegel called in the Preface to the *Phenomenology* a thought-determination, indeed a major one.

The other major antecedent is not Kant but Fichte, whom Hegel regards as completing the Kantian system by adding both a self-consciously reflective development of pure reason and a movement of interdetermination through the interplay of I and not-I.

In a rejection of the Hegelian claim that Schelling conducted his philosophical education in public, Heidegger has written: "there is seldom a thinker who has fought so passionately ever since his earliest times for his one and unique standpoint as Schelling did."[3] This interpretation has exerted much salutary influence on contemporary Schelling scholarship, as has Heidegger's remark that Schelling is the boldest and most far-reaching thinker of German Idealism and that in adhering rigorously to the unfolding of German Idealism, Schelling has driven it beyond itself. However, when Hegel's lectures on Schelling are reread in light of these comments, one is led back to the very turning point of which Heidegger speaks.

Hegel accomplishes a thoroughly scrupulous scholarly undertaking in his detailing of Schelling's discourses from their beginning, and one is convinced by his readings—up to the point where they cease to be a matter of conscientious exposition. Hegel notes Schelling's first beginning in a "literally" (*wörtlich*) Fichtean work in which Fichte's self-reflective "I" serves as both principle and demonstration. In his 1797 and 1798 works, Schelling is said to develop a philosophy of nature from Kantian principles, but expressed in a Fichtean manner. In "more recent" publications according to Hegel, Schelling accomplishes a major development and deserves to be called the first genuine exponent of a philosophy of nature. He also asserts: "Schelling's Philosophy must be still viewed as conceived in its evolution."[4] Finally, he speaks of the 1809 *Freiheitsschrift* as "of a deep and speculative kind; however, it stands uniquely on its own (*einzeln für sich*), and in philosophy nothing can stand alone."[5]

Thus, it has been a serious misreading of Hegel to ascribe negative judgments to his contemporary. He saw the evolution of Schelling's thought as a positive development for the unfolding of philosophy in the crucial modern age where, according to Hegel, spirit has arrived at full self-consciousness, and world history as the history of partial shapes has come to a close. His critique of Schelling could hardly consist of greater honor: Schelling's is the penultimate thought of the history of philosophy. As early as 1801, in his *Differenz des Fichteschen und Schellingschen*

Systems der Philosophie, Hegel declares Schelling's advance over the Fichtean system in terms that analogically anticipate Hegel's own classic formulations: where both thinkers posited a fundamental unity of subject and object, Fichte's subjective subject-object found further and deeper expression in Schelling's objective subject-object.

In case there could be any doubt, consider the following: "[Schelling's] system is the latest, most interesting true form of philosophy that we had to consider. The idea iteslf, that the true is the concrete, has been elevated (*herausheben*): it is the unity of subjective and objective. Every stage has its own form in the system: the ultimate stage is the totality of the forms. The second great achievement (*Grosse*) of Schelling consists of his having demonstrated the forms of spirit in his philosophy of nature."[6] What remained missing in Schelling and thus in need of completion is *logic*, in which the idea itself finds itself free of all else. If it makes sense to speak of what is present in Schelling that must be negated in the final stage, *imagination* must be purified. The difference, put in terms of simple opposition is that for Schelling, the highest manifestation of spirit is the work of art; for Hegel, the work of art must be surpassed in logic.

One fateful consequence of Hegelian thought is the relegation of ancient philosophy to a moment that has been *aufgehoben*, preserved, but transformed and surpassed. According to his *Aesthetics*, the work of art did serve as the locus of truth, and truth made itself manifest in *beauty*, the shining of being. Of Greek sculpture, Hegel wrote: "Nothing is or could ever be more beautiful."[7] However, he also declares the death of art. This matter is all too quickly dismissed. His claim is that art no longer commands obeisance as it once did. The god is no longer in the temple. One no longer bends the knee before the representation of the Madonna. Reason now rules, along with the institutions and the outlook that derive from it. The danger that Hegel's *Aesthetics* seeks to avoid is the sinking of art to a matter of mere amusement and opinion. Just as the history of philosophy is in truth the unfolding of the *one* philosophy in the manner that it necessarily had to unfold, so too the stages of art necessarily took their places in history as they had to. The science of aesthetics is precisely the presentation of those stages, recollecting them for the sake of the present.

However this might serve to present the unfolding of art through human history, the deed of declaring the pastness of art—the death of art—even in Hegel's quite special sense disqualifies art from providing a paradigm for the future. This applies with particular force to Greek art, upon which Schelling continued to draw and upon which drawing *we* draw in Schelling's wake. In this sense, the much-abused word *life* takes on renewed significance. The science of aesthetics presented by Hegel in which the dead past is undergone recollectively takes place beside a philosophy of art that projects the same past toward a living and thus yet unanticipated future.

In Schelling, the archaic excavation becomes explicit for the first time. With one extraordinary exception, his early essays had an expressly Fichtean stamp, and this stamp occurs until what might be called his gradual liberation from the Fichtean problematic is complete. This excavation takes place implicitly and is enacted from a standpoint that would seem to work against both the metaphorics and the deed of digging in the earth, namely, *system building*. Fichte's *Wissenschaftslehre* is Kantianism made systematic in its author's own eyes. The Kantian "I," most especially in its practical function as *act*, provides the high point of the system. Fichte grants Spinozism its completeness, but finds it entirely insufficient because it cannot and does not account for consciousness, and on account of its determinism it cannot account for even the most mundane human behaviors. Fichte writes: "Spinoza could not have been in a state of conviction, not believe it, for it stood in the most immediate contradiction in daily life, where he was bound to regard himself as free and independent."[8]

What, then, can one say about Fichte—also about Kant—with regard to the archaic soundings heard in the Spinoza interpretation above? They have accomplished the following. By acknowledging the limits of reason, they have implicitly pointed to a region where reason cannot reach. In other words, the gap between the "is" of theoretical reason, which restricts being to its appearance in sensible intuition, and the "ought" of unconditional practical obligation, opens into a realm that is *other*. It must also be said that Kant's *Critique of Judgment* did not hold compelling interest for Fichte. In this, one could write a *Differenzschrift* of another kind, in which Fichte's practical Kantianism is contrasted with Schelling's aesthetic Kantianism.

Many years ago and with a thoroughly different purpose in mind, I unconsciously wrote a brief *Differenzschrift* along such lines. With Schiller standing in for the Kant of the third Critique, my essay titled "The Precise Kantian Origin of the Fichte–Schiller Conflict" treated Schiller's rejection of Fichte's essay "Über Geist und Buchstab in der Philosophie" as a dispute of the most genuine philosophical nature,[9] rather than as tainted by personal motives (as the literature had treated it). After reading Fichte's essay (which had not been translated at the time), it seems clear to me. First, Fichte contributed an excellent essay, in which he presented his view of philosophy in terms governed by his Kant interpretation in terms of which "The Primacy of the Practical" served as his quite appropriate anchor. In retrospect, one can say that it certainly deserved publication.

The suspicion that parts of it could be read as thinly veiled attacks on Schiller's *Ästhetische Briefe* may have played a role, but such speculation can provide nothing definitive. The Kantian texts can, however. The *Ästhetische Briefe* treated the *Critique of Judgment* as its template, and regarded the axis on which humanity turned on what he called the play-impulse (*Spieltrieb*). The play-impulse alone is free in the pure sense. The two other impulses operate under certain constrains. The form- or reason-impulse operates primarily in order to determine the limits governing the moral realm, while the matter-impulse operates in order to seek pathological satisfaction. That is, his taking the three critiques together and locating the third at its center animate Schiller's Kantianism. By contrast, Fichte regards the three impulses animating Kantianism somewhat differently: knowledge-impulse, practical-impulse, and aesthetic-impulse, with the first two in clear priority.

It is hardly surprising that a strong case can be made for either interpretation. If one finds the determinative judgments to be decisive, and reflective judgments to be their nonconceptual subordinates, then the Fichtean view will find favor. If one sees reflective judgments as implicitly underpinning all cognition by virtue of their alignment of the subjective faculties, then Schelling's Kantianism will have its clear appeal. And no common ground appears available to settle such a dispute. But the question here concerns Schelling: how does Schelling stand in such an argument?

While it may appear that Schelling begins from a Fichtean stance to a stance that resembles Schiller's, I strongly suggest that this can be the case only superficially. That is, from the beginning Schelling's thought has been driven by subterranean archaic sources that can never become fully explicit by their very nature. Even when they surface and recede in his texts, even when they seem to become available through nonrational origins and means, they remain veiled—productively veiled. In other words, Hegel's claim that Schelling undertook his philosophical education in public (with the *Freiheitsschrift* being somehow unique), and Heidegger's claim that no thinker has proceeded so consistently from his one unique standpoint, are both defensible in their own terms. However, we who think today encounter a Schelling whose strangeness exceeds both formulations, and requires a different approach—or rather, a different organ of apprehension.

In what follows, I will attempt to *hear* those archaic resonances in Schelling. I shall follow the chronological path of his works with an ear toward discerning those resonances. In each, I shall mark one or two places where the soundings are to take place, and record what can be heard there. These soundings will show how the thinkers around him at that most fertile period of philosophy, as well as their noble predecessors in modern philosophy, have concealed the darkness out of which they emerged and which made them possible at all.

Notes

1. Georg Wilhelm Friedrich Hegel, *Logik, Erster Teil* (Berlin: Felix Meiner, 1971), 31.
2. Ibid., 22.
3. Martin Heidegger, *Schellings Abhandlung Über das Wesen der menschlichen Freiheit (1809)* (Tübingen: Max Niemeyer, 1971), 7.
4. Georg Wilhelm Friedrich Hegel, *Vorlesungen über der Geschichte der Philosophie*, vol. 3 (Leipzig: Phillip Reklam, 1971), 617.
5. Ibid., 619.
6. Ibid., 621.
7. Georg Wilhelm Friedrich Hegel, *Aesthetics*, 2 vols., trans. T. M. Knox (Oxford: Oxford University Press, 1975), 1:517.
8. Johann Gottlieb Fichte, *The Science of Knowledge*, trans. Peter Heath and John Lachs (Cambridge: Cambridge University Press, 1982), 81. It puzzles me that there is no better translation of the 1794 *Grundlage der gesamten Wissenschaftslehre* than the available ones, which are dreadful in my opinion. *Wissenschaftslehre* can be straightforwardly translated as "Doctrine of Science." Still worse, Heath and Lachs render "Das Ich" as "the self," when Fichte is clearly linking the term with Kant's transcendental use of it. The above citation, accurately translated by Heath and Lachs, comes from the "Second Introduction to the *Wissenschaftslehre*," 1:513.
9. In *7. Internationaler Kant-Kongresses, Akten II.2., Mainz 1990* (Bonn: Bouvier, 1991), 523–534.

3 Unruly Greek Schelling

The "extraordinary exception" to which I referred above is Schelling's very first publication titled *Über Mythen, historische Sagen und Philosopheme der ältesten Welt* (Concerning Myths, Historical Sages, and Philosophemes of the Oldest World) (1793).[1] There is nothing Spinozist, Kantian, or Fichtean in it at all. Perhaps the eighteen-year-old Schelling had not yet read them. However, the essay exhibits both a great deal of confidence and often-uncanny prescience regarding what was to come. In a peculiar way, it also bears upon the way of this subterranean exploration, in that the first section under the heading "Value and Character of Mythical History" begins with a section titled "Oral Tradition," in which *hearing* plays the leading role. On one hand, "hearing is not the clearest and most explicit (*deutlichst*) among the senses"; however on the other, "no other means were available for the oldest humans to provide education" (I, 4, 44).[2] While we have only a "weak reverberation of that pure, original voice in the written documents of the people," (I, 8, 48) and while there are differences in what sounds to the ear in these voices among different peoples in different regions, what is said in them remains the same among every people and in every region.

Later in the essay, Schelling distinguishes between mythical philosophy that has been handed down orally and the philosophy that occurs more rigorously in writing by claiming that the former lacks the precision of the latter. However, he also notes that the philosophy handed down "from father to son" has the following quality, which will surface more and more in his own later and more precise philosophy: "Oral philosophy is more fiery, richer, and more lively when compared with the employment of writing by human beings accustomed to a colder, more patient, more persistent investigation; the former seduces (*überredet*) more, the latter convinces more; the former is more delightful, the latter is more instructive; the former is attributed to imagination, the latter is attributed to understanding" (I, I, 4).

In a fascinating footnote on Plato, he comments regarding its sensible presentation that "one often travels with him in a certain chiaroscuro (*Helldunkel*) full of presentiments of truth, often basing his sublime concepts more upon presentiment-like (*ahnend*) feelings than upon clear knowledge" (I, 29, 69). These two passages serve both to distinguish and to relate two ways of language. It is fair to say that the youthful Schelling hit upon a matter that will recur throughout his thought, not coming to its ultimate creative transformation until the 1809 *Freiheitsschrift*.

This ambiguity in language shows itself also in his account of mythical history, which one can call both clear and convoluted at once. A philosopheme, as Schelling employs the term, refers to a Greek mythological account within which philosophical material occurs. Most noteworthy is Schelling's alliance of mythos with truth. The word *mythos* can be extended such that mythical history is true history. Schelling writes: "A history that is made sensible (*versinnlicht*) by means of some truth can be true history, at least according to its principal conditions. Insofar as in a mythical philosopheme the meaning of mythos can be extended to true history, a truth in the ancient world is made sensible" by its means. Mythical philosophemes can everywhere and in general also be so named (I, 31, 71).

We can say that before he begins to wrestle expressly with Kant, Fichte, and Hegel, Schelling's thought has already engaged with what I shall call matters of *excavation* and *depth*. The ways of access must always involve *hearing* and *seeing*. The mythemes and philosophemes of ancient times can never be buried or surpassed, but always speak to us in our every effort to seek wisdom. Therefore, the task involves not only and not fundamentally the interpretation of the ancient sayings into our terms, that is, the measure of these sayings as they might be regarded preconceptually. Rather, the principal task consists of *letting them speak in their own way*, that is, first and foremost, letting them occur as the ciphers that they are.

Schelling mentions two contemporaries who thought that Prometheus was an actual person.[3] Against this view as well as against the view that the Greek poets borrow their images only from "the simple life of the primal fathers (*Urväter*) for the sake of description of the Golden Age," Schelling writes: "Nevertheless I am convinced that the Greek mythos of Prometheus and Pandora is nothing more and nothing less than a poetized mythos of a sensualization (*Versinnlichung*) of a philosophical speculation made sensible" (I, 15, 55n). *Speculation* here has the Greek sense of *theoria* as beholding. What is beheld in this ancient beholding cannot be a mere mimetic representation of limits imposed by the preconceptual status of its historical epoch. Rather, this speculation includes within itself what will later be thought in a deeper manner as the twofold in God giving birth to himself.

For the remainder of this section, I will employ aspects of Hegel's sequential treatment of Schelling's work that I praised above; however, I shall seek out traces that diverge significantly and fatefully from this account. In this way, I hope to make the anterior undertones of modern philosophy audible, undertones that have been concealed beneath its apparent hegemony of reason. In addition, I shall treat Schelling's 1802 *Philosophy of Art*, where the Greek presence, so apparent on the surface, still dwells in its depths.

Vom Ich als Prinzip der Philosophie oder Über das Unbedingte im menschlichen Wissen (1795)

While this work can clearly be seen for nearly all intents as an expository take on Fichte's appropriation of Kant's *Critique of Pure Reason* in his 1794 *Grundlage der gesamten Wissenschaftslehre*, one tantalizing short section occurs that does not fall explicitly within the overall project. It concerns *language* and its relation to the notion of intellectual intuition: "I want my language to be akin to that of Plato, or to that of his kindred spirit Jacobi, in order to be able to distinguish the absolute unchangeable being from each conditioned, changeable existence. But I see that when these men themselves want to speak of the unchangeable and supersensible, they struggle with their language—and I think that that absolute in us is not chained through any mere word in a human language, and that only self-achieved (*selbsterrungenes*) intuiting of the intellectual in us comes to the aid of the piecework of our language" (I, I, 216).

Leaving aside the validity of Schelling's Plato interpretation on this matter, the discourse here points to a differentiation of language and thought. For Kant, thought is *judgment*, that is, it is clearly propositional. The "little word of relation" (*Verhähtniswörtchen*) "is" in every judgment binds the subject to the predicate by means of the necessary transcendental unity of apperception. As a committed Kantian at the time of the

Grundlage, Fichte shared this view. In this very brief section marked off at the end of §15 of the *Critique of Pure Reason*, however, Schelling suggests a breach between self-achieved intuition and the language that, in its attempt to articulate it, finds itself falling short.

This breach between not only thought but also thought and *language* is peculiar to Schelling, and exemplifies such peculiarities that will continue to occur. To be sure, this one retains a Kantian–Fichtean twist. Ultimately, all of our singular knowledge bifurcates into the objects we know and those that we will: "the beginning and the end of your knowledge is the same—there, intuition, here belief (*Glaube!*)" (I, I, 216). However, the intuition/language split remains and will play a major role as Schelling's thought develops. At this early stage, this split foreshadows the underlying *disorder* out of which anything like "unity" may be fashioned.

In comparison with the philosophy of other thinkers, in Schelling the breach between thought and language grows ever more explicit and even thematic as his philosophy develops.

First Outline of a System of the Philosophy of Nature (1799)

If it were possible for a modern work to appear archaic in its own terms, Schelling's *First Outline of a System of the Philosophy of Nature* would surely qualify. The content is driven by the notion of a chasm within identity that enables the peculiar deduction of the a priori notions of both chemistry and physics. Perhaps the most accessible entry to this very difficult text is found in a late section of the shorter 1801 version, where Schelling writes:

> Our aim, in view of this object, is to separate science and empiricism as soul and body, and by admitting nothing into science that is not of an *a priori* construction, to strip empiricism of all theory, and restore it to its original nakedness.
>
> The opposition between empiricism and science rests therefore on this: that the former regards its object in *being*, as something prepared and accomplished; science, on the other hand, views its object as *becoming*, and as something that has yet to be accomplished.[4]

It would be difficult to locate a more dramatic reversal than Schelling's in which what might be called the distinctive signature of science finds its proper correlate in *becoming*. How might this be understood? Perhaps the most promising approach involves a reinterpretation of the Kantian a priori. As noted in the previous section, the word "is" in every judgment binds the subject to the predicate by means of the necessary transcendental unity of apperception. However, the purification of special metaphysics from the realm of objective validity by critique functions at once to limit knowledge to appearances, that is, to the empirical. Only those judgments that occur in the empirical region operate as *being*.

For Kant's theoretical philosophy, the Principles of the Pure Understanding comprise the entirety of the a priori. These Principles, which are always already functioning in every human apprehension, are composed of the Categories (Understanding), the Schemata (Imagination), and pure intuition. While all three elements play a necessary role, imagination as the function of synthesis deserves special attention here. With respect to the Ideas of reason in special metaphysics, imagination can effect no valid synthesis; only *possible* objects, that is, objects that can belong to intuition, fall within the scope of valid synthesis. To place this in terms of Schelling's reversal, the *science* of the so-humbled metaphysics must concern itself only with objects given in *time*, the form of all intuition—that is, this science must concern itself with *becoming*.

A rethinking of the Kantian a priori in light of the above has the following surprising result: since the Kantian a priori must be oriented toward becoming, and since only empirical judgments have being as their status, then the Kantian a priori itself can be neither becoming nor being. Could it be that Schelling's lifelong meditation on the *chora* of Plato's *Timaeus*—the receptacle that is neither being nor becoming but that allows anything like being and becoming to show themselves at all—instinctively aligns with the Kantian a priori? The *chora* never shows its face, nor do the Principles taken collectively as the conditions for the possibility of experience. The latter are the *necessary* conditions. The *chora* does not make itself manifest until the *Timaeus*'s second beginning, the beginning from necessity, has occurred. However, the anterior *chora* has been present throughout.

What makes this thought particularly provocative is Schelling's introduction of Indifference (*Indifferenz*) as a "third" principle between identity and difference. "Basic principle (*Hauptsatz*): No identity of nature is absolute, every identity is only indifference" (III, 309, 309). In the footnote to this principle, Schelling explains that opposition (*Gegensatz*) can be opposition "only through that striving for identity" (III, 309,

309n). When measured against his later work, this early account of indifference can be seen as only preliminary. Indifference presents itself as murky, indistinct, even confused.

However, indifference by its very nature must be spoken of in this manner, much as access to the *chora* is said by Timeaus to be "difficult" (*chalepon*). In this first outline, indifference is described as always partial—one might call it *local*. It recollects the Fichtean notion of striving but in a manner that transcends the Fichtean problematic. By contrast to the identity that opposition always strives toward, opposition is also infinite "*so that again only mediated members of the synthesis that can never itself produce the absolute synthesis . . . but [arrive] always at only relative indifference points* and every emergent indifference leaves a new opposition that again passes over into indifference" (II, III, 310). That is to say, indifference in this outline cannot yet be called fully anterior.

Keith R. Peterson performs an immense service with his translation of *First Outline of a System of the Philosophy of Nature*. His acute "Introduction" situates this text as it emerges from its Kantian heritage and locates its place within Schelling's work as a whole in a well-thought-out manner. Even more remarkably, he provides an excellent rendering of a work that was untimely when it appeared and is yet more distant from us now. Therefore, I feel ungracious—churlish, even—to criticize what seems to me to be an especially poor and misleading choice. I refer to his rendering of *Kunsttrieb* as "technical drive." As Schelling ascribes this impulse to animals, one can understand a translator's perplexity when confronted with it. However, this locution clearly denotes "artistic impulse."

In keeping with the result of the previous section, for Schelling this often regarded "third"—after the lawfulness of reason and the pathology of sensation—stands *first in actu*. Further, the word was understood as *art-drive* in Schelling's time. First and foremost among them, Schelling unmistakably employs the language of art rather than the language of technique to characterize this impulse:

> It is not enough that the products of this drive themselves confirm this view far more evidently than [the] analogy with reason. All products of the art-drive (*Kunsttrieb*) have the peculiarity that they are perfect in kind and are genuine masterpieces (*lauter Meisterstücke*). Every animal that has such a drive steps onto the stage with its art

and is born cultivated (*unterreichtet*). Nothing here is half, incomplete, or requiring improvement. However, just as the incomplete is at once the perfectible, the complete is necessarily at once the Imperfectible. *Imperfectability* (*Imperfectibilität*) is therefore the principal characteristic of all of the artistic products of animals. (Trans. 131, orig. II, III, 181)[5]

By *Imperfectibilität*, Schelling clearly explains its sense: there is simply no possibility of improvement given the nature of the animal's art-drive since the latter always hits its mark as precisely as its nature allows. He does not deny that there is some analogy to reason that is easily perceptible to the human eye, but does not ascribe such an analogy to the animal.

The art-drive of animals culminates in the *regularity* of its products. The visible product cannot be other than it is, because the inner force of the animal exhausts itself in its production. Some animals, especially insects, expire shortly after their productive capacity is spent. "Now, in organic forms we only observe products in which everything is reciprocally means and end. We have no other name but *organic* for this kind of inner perfection, because organic nature is a *unity* with respect to it.— Where the organic formation (*Bildung*) stands at its limit and the organic force extends out beyond this limit it no longer produces inner perfection but only outer perfection" (trans. 134, II, III, 186).

Regarding geometry, it is clear that in the motions of the planets (and in the laws of motions generally), nature is "the most perfect geometer" (trans. 134, II, III, 186). It performs its motions from blind necessity. However, Schelling's "blind necessity" cannot be understood too quickly. For example, no mere animal can produce a hexagon, and it can be rightly said that the hexagon is a product of necessity. However, this product must be understood as the externalization of the art-drive beyond the limit of the *organic* form of a rational being. What, then, do we behold when we look out at nature and everywhere find order and regularity, just as we find it in the laws of geometry and of motion? "You see your own understanding in nature, so it seems to you to produce *for you*. And so you are only right to see its lawful productions as an analogue of freedom, *because even unconditioned necessity becomes freedom once more*" (II, III, 186).

This analysis introduces a subtle and distinctive element into the discourse on freedom and necessity that can be best approached by recourse to the early Greek *Anagkē*. I recall the consideration above of Parmenides, Fragment 298, that reads:

> The same (*tauton*) and in the same (*en tautō*) it lies on its same (*heauton*) and thus fixed it will stay. For strong Necessity (*Anagkē*) has it imprisoned (*desmoisin*) in a limit (*peiratos*) that keeps it confined within.[6]

Again, Parmenidean Necessity must be heard in terms of its *anteriority* to all other concerns. Necessity's imprisonment of *estin* as *tauton* must be heard as its *gift* through which Being may draw the thought of those under its sway toward it.

As we have also seen in terms of the Greek mythos, *Anagkē*, present at the creation of the cosmos and so without parents, dwells outside any causal connection. As mother of the Fates, who mete out the destinies of human beings, she may be seen retrospectively as the *Urbild* from which all other images belonging to the human things derive. Recalling this context further, from the Myth of Er, the soul of the human being chooses a *daimon* rather than the reverse. This mythos can be heard both echoing beneath the modern context and, in a way, sounding ahead of it. For in the modern context, causality takes its place among the indispensable concepts. For Schelling's systematic thought, which always remains Greek in its endeavor to actualize the Heraclitean *hen panta einai*, one finds a coming together of Greek mythos and modern, presumably nonmythical, causality.

I hesitate to call this coming together a *synthesis*, both because the word is loaded with accumulated sediment and because it suggests that two separate strains of philosophizing were first separate and then later combined. Schelling's distinction among even his closest colleagues among the "German Idealist" thinkers is and remains the thoroughgoing and original unity of which the interpenetration of Greek and Modern is its outcome. The *First Outline of a System of the Philosophy of Nature* seems to be presented in predominantly causal terms. However, the primal unity of the system cannot be accounted for causally any more than the Greek *Anagkē* can. The latter is its silent undergirding, yet this silence yields its sense to the attentive ear.

Here, at the point of the *Kunsttrieb* at which unconditioned necessity becomes freedom, we experience both the high point and the flow from the high point of what Schelling understands as *nature* in the scientific sense, that is, nature as the anterior a priori ground of the science of speculative physics (which is ultimately identical with the philosophy of nature) and of chemistry, its material branch. Our ascription of rationality in the animal world, or at least of an analogy to reason, bears witness to freedom as the essence of reason. In the 1809 *Freiheitsschrift*, Schelling will speak of the "contradiction" of freedom and necessity as the animating provocation for all genuine science. In the *First Outline*, this contradiction finds itself concealed under the art-drive.

Also concealed is the "organ" of this drive, namely, *imagination*. Schelling's supremely gifted contemporary Schiller conceived the art-drive as the central force to which both the rational-drive (*Vernunfttrieb*) and the sense-drive (*Sinntrieb*) are subordinate. To be sure, Schiller's thought derived almost entirely from Kant's critical philosophy, and for Schiller the art-drive, also called the *play-drive*, was not discussed in terms of its products in the way Schelling discusses it. Whereas for Kant and Schiller the architectonic aim results in an articulation having its origin in the subjective faculties of the mind, for Schelling there is one system, the system of the whole that is articulated through the one unconditioned principle. This unconditioned principle of the whole is manifest in nature as one elucidation and is manifest as a spirit in the other elucidation.

System of Transcendental Idealism (1800)

This work presents an elucidation of the system from the side of spirit, yet it hardly mirrors the *First Outline*. It recapitulates many Kantian and Fichtean themes, albeit in new settings. Contradiction is no longer concealed within the art-drive, but rather it is asserted repeatedly that contradiction alone drives transcendental idealism. One finds no mention of an art-drive. However, the conception of systematic completeness includes a dimension not found in Kant or in Fichte. For Kant, the kind of judgment belonging to aesthetic experience, called reflective judgment, is sharply distinguished from determinant judgment. The former's validity can attain only a subjective universality, while determinant judgments attain objective universality as well. One finds no such distinction in Schelling.

This 1800 treatise is a remarkable work in many respects. As in the philosophy of nature, unconscious processes play a major role, but these are intertwined with consciousness, often in complex ways. The role of freedom becomes expanded even beyond the lofty peak on which it resided for Kant and Fichte. That is, it belongs to the unconditioned highest principle from which, as we have seen, nature is deduced as its necessary unfolding into externality. Spirit, or the unfolding of self-conscious reason, is that side of the principle from which internality and its products come into being. Though Schelling often speaks in Fichtean language, that is, he speaks of the "I" (*das Ich*) and "wavering" or "hovering" (*Schweben*), there is a decided drift in usage from the language of ought (*Sollen*) to the language of Being (*Sein*) and from an emphasis on finitude to the necessary presupposition of infinitude.

One can easily discern Schelling's Spinozist roots. With them, one can also hear those echoes of the Greek undertones of Spinoza's thought exposed in the previous section, even as he adopts the language of critical philosophy. However, these Greek undertones sound more distinctly in the deduction of art from the highest principle. Though Schelling does not once explicitly mention Greek art or archaic Greek thought, one cannot read this section of the work without these coming to mind. I shall work backward from this deduction to the treatment of imagination in order to demonstrate this sounding.

The primary distinction driving the deduction is "the identity of the conscious and the unconscious in the 'I,' and the consciousness of this identity" (trans. 219, II, III, 612). While here Schelling seems to employ Fichtean language, it should be borne in mind that philosophy is always *productive*. That is, receptivity does not belong to it essentially—all is action. Nature occurs as unconscious production. Intellect, insofar as it thinks nature, occurs as conscious production. Schelling's division of actions results in the requirement that there be unity for the "I," and at the same time separation, in order for consciousness to be aware of its production. Thus he asks: "How is this contradiction to be resolved?" (trans. 220, II, III, 614).

This unity/separation duplicity might well be seen as a radical reinterpretation of Kant's spontaneity/receptivity division. Without Kant's a priori apparatus, namely, transcendental apperception and the principles, no experience is possible at all. This apparatus is always already at work. In Schelling's language, it is the unconscious and infinite genesis of consciousness itself. By its means alone, consciousness can become self-reflective. Nevertheless, it is inconceivable that this act takes place outside of its products. That is, in speech one can separate the a priori apparatus from its products, but in actuality the products always stand opposite consciousness. One never experiences merely the empty apparatus.

In the apprehension of the product (the object) by consciousness, the reconciliation of the contradictory elements occurs in a striking fashion. Schelling writes of this: "Now since it was the free tendency to self-intuition, the feeling accompanying this intuition will be that of an infinite satisfaction (*Befriedigung*). With the completion of the product, all urge to produce comes to rest (*still stehen*), all contradictions are resolved, all riddles solved" (trans. 221, II, III, 615). At this point in the text, Schelling is not explicit about the product that would result in such a feeling of infinite satisfaction. In a way, almost any object that one might call "empirical" in Kant's language might qualify. One might infer that the process by which one judges, for example, that "all bodies are extended," has an unshakable quietude out of which such an insight can be articulated at all. There is nothing in Schelling's text that expressly rules this out. The latter is a consequence of his collapsing the distinction between determinative and reflective judgments.

However, he retains the special significance of the work of art and of the role of genius from Kant, albeit in a different manner. Schelling prepares his approach by means of following out his original unconscious/conscious unity/separation duplicities. First, he declares that in case the originally free movement culminates in a product such that the *appearance* of freedom with which it originated is removed, what remains is wondrous:

> [The intelligence] will feel itself surprised and *delighted* (*beglückt*) by this unification, i.e., will look upon it as a free-willed (*freiwillig*) gift of a higher nature that has made the impossible possible.
>
> This unknown, however, that here puts objective and conscious activity in unexpected harmony is nothing other than the absolute that contains the universal ground of the pre-established harmony between the conscious and the unconscious. (trans. 221, II, III, 615)

However, this harmony differs significantly from the Kantian harmony of imagination and understanding in the reflective judgment of beauty. The product, Schelling says, radiates back (*widerstrahlt*) and is "destiny for the one who acts, i.e., a dark unknown power (*Gewalt*) that completes (*hinzubringt*) the perfected and the objective to the piecework of freedom" (trans. 222, II, III, 616). It belongs to the nature of destiny that it cannot be envisaged or represented as such, but requires in a certain way the cooperation with that freedom to which it must stand opposed. This odd cooperation of dispersion and unity, Schelling writes, is characterized by "the dark (*dunkel*) concept of *genius*" (trans. 222, II, III, 616).

Why must genius be called dark? For Kant, genius is surely rare, but is said to stand in for the ordinary place of a concept; the place of the latter is taken by "aesthetic ideas," which cannot in principle be brought to language but that make themselves manifest in original works of art. For Schelling, the work of art has an objective nature that derives from the initial unity of unconscious and conscious out of which all things flow. "The product we postulate is none other than the product of genius, or, since genius is possible only in the arts, *the art-product* (*Kunstprodukt*)" (trans. 223, II, III, 616). But Schelling's notion of destiny differentiates him clearly from Kant, as does his notion of the absolute. Destiny (*Schicksal*) links Schelling expressly to his early Greek forebears.

Schelling's implicit notion of destiny (he offers no definition or elucidation) recollects, in its own way, the Platonic sense discussed above. By this I mean that in Plato, one does not find notions that come forth until much later: consciousness (and unconsciousness), concept versus intuition, proofs for the existence of God, divisions between "branches" of philosophy, and the like. Nor does the idea of freedom play anything like the role it does for Schelling, if indeed one can properly speak of an "idea of freedom" at all in the Platonic dialogues. However, the Platonic mythos does include the notion of choice—the soul in Hades chooses its *daimon* rather than having the Fates choose one for it—which approaches Kant's moral law as the *ratio essendi* of freedom and Schelling's appropriation of Kant's notion of freedom only at a great distance.

However, the mythical openness of the cycle of souls in Hades sounds an echo in Schelling's "destiny." Just as mythical necessity (*Anagkē*) shows itself in regard to our notion of efficient causality, so to do the mythical fates (*Moirai*) show themselves to be anterior to any spontaneous causality. In Schelling, just as the art-drive forms a bridge to freedom in its highest manifestation, so too does the aesthetic product form a bridge to destiny. The wonder belonging to Schelling's notion of destiny consists in its location beyond and outside of the scope of reason and even of transcendental idealism. It would not nearly suffice to reformulate or reorient human thought either back to its Greek origin or within its modern manifestation. Schelling himself seems to admit that *he* could not find membership within his own ultimate sense of destiny.

This is because philosophy in his time had to generate itself out of that original opposition, on one side to philosophy and on the other to art. In its *archē*, philosophy flowed from and found nourishment in poetry, and to this origin it must finally return. Philosophy finds its completion in its origin, that is, the breach will be healed in and by *mythology*: "But how a new mythology is itself to arise, which shall be the invention (*Erfindung*), not of some individual author but of a represented new race (*ein neuen vorstellenden Geschlechts*), not, as it were, of only One poet (*nur Einen Dichter*)—that is a problem whose solution can be looked for only in the future destinies of the world, and in the course of histories to come" (trans. 233, II, III, 629).

How are we to understand this most unorthodox formulation that sounds so unusual, if not wayward, to our contemporary ears? First of all, one can hardly find a more decisive differentiation from the thought of Hegel, whether one considers Schelling's work as a step on the way to its fulfillment in Hegel or as the farthest-reaching and deepest thinker of his time (as Heidegger does, and as I do, but for somewhat different reasons).

That is to say, it is not the phenomenology of spirit. More to the point of the question, however, all the components of Schelling's remarkable saying point back to his Greek underpinnings and must be regarded as a projection of these underpinnings toward a yet to be thought future. In the widest sense, we may say that the Heraclitean "one is all" (*hen panta*) becomes reinterpreted as a future for which "all is one." However, for Schelling this future does not occur as the working out systematically of the mythical Greek heritage in which the otherness of the Greek mythos becomes subsumed within spirit as self-conscious reason. A new race is needed, in order for a return to philosophy to return appropriately to its source. What does the Greek mythos say concerning races of human beings?

One need not look far. In *Works and Days*, Hesiod sings of five races of human beings: a golden race under Chronos "who lived like gods without sorrow of heart, remote and free from toil and grief"; a race "less noble by far" ruled by Zeus, slow to grow, stupid when full-grown, sorrowful, and unmindful of Zeus (who eliminated them) and the other gods; third came the bronze race, which "was in no way equal to the silver age, but was terrible and strong. They loved the lamentable works of Ares and deeds of violence," and destroyed itself with its own bronze weaponry. Zeus then made a heroic race, "a god-like race of hero-men who are called demi-gods, the race before our own, throughout the boundless earth," who died on the battlefields of Troy and Thebes and passed on to the Elysian fields. This is the only race of humans that is not named by a metal.

Finally comes the iron race, Hesiod's own race. This race images its metal in the sense that iron is the *cheapest* of the group. "There will be no favor for the man who keeps his oath or for the just or for the good; but rather men will praise the evil-doer and his violent dealing. Strength will be right and reverence will cease to be."[7] The poet sings of his wish to be born during the age before and the (not yet existing) subsequent age, because in the age of Iron both Aidos (goddess of shame) and Nemesis will leave the earth and thus human beings to their own mostly wretched devices and join the blessed immortal gods.

Therefore, Schelling regards his "Iron Age" time as a time of transition, and his race—though he keeps silent on it—as a historical pivot, that is, a race of reason in the process of exceeding itself. This is the sense of the following provocative claim: "Philosophy attains, to be sure, the highest, but it brings to this summit only, so to say, a fragment (*Brückstück*) of a man. Art brings *the whole man*, as he is, to that point, namely to a knowledge of the highest, and this is what underlies the eternal difference and the wonder of art" (trans. 233, II, III, 630).

Schelling's time is frequently called a time of bifurcation (*Entzweiung*) by the thinkers gathered under the umbrella of German Idealism. The "bi-" of bifurcation makes itself manifest not only in the dualisms that have taken various forms since Descartes's supposed dualism of *res cogitans* and *res extensa*. But the very acknowledgment of bifurcation adumbrates a unity from which the twoness emerges. For Hegel, this unity is already inscribed into the history of consciousness as external necessity and into the science of logic as internal necessity. The unity is ultimately a unity of self-reflected reason having come home to itself.

For Schelling, however, the unity is *anticipated*, that is, while it can be glimpsed, it has yet to arrive. Nor is this unity ultimately rational; it is nonrational in the sense that it is primarlily *aesthetic*. Hence, rational human beings such as Schelling and Hegel, not to mention the varied and sundry "rationalists" and "empiricists" both learned and unlearned, cannot obtain membership under the sway of this new unity. What might this race be like? How would it differ from "us"? A hint is provided at the conclusion of Schelling's 1802 *Lectures concerning the Method of Academic Studies*, in which he holds up the unified, communal life of the ancient Greeks as an exemplar for the modern era and, by extension, of the proposed new race of men.

What draws the thought of Schelling forward to the anticipated unity is that which he hears in the Greek past. Remarkably, philosophy receives no mention in the "One" living artwork. Surely there can be no doubt, given the very many instances of praise for philosophy as the highest manifestation of thought throughout Schelling's texts, that nothing other than philosophy drives him. Nor can there be any doubt that Greek philosophy expressly lives in Schelling's thought. Why, then, is philosophy excluded from the image of classical Greece in the citation above? Will "the new race of human beings" have no need of philosophy?

Philosophy of Art (1802)

Early in his introduction, Schelling asserts the kind of art with which he will concern himself, sharply distinguishing it from any nominal designations: "I am speaking of a more sacred art, one that in the words of antiquity is a tool of the gods, a proclaimer of divine mysteries, the unveiler of the ideas: I am speaking of that unborn beauty whose undesecrated radiance only dwells in and illuminates purer souls, and whose form is just as concealed from and inaccessible to the sensual eye as the truth corresponding to it. Nothing of that which a baser sensibility calls art can concern the philosopher."[8] With this vivid stroke, Schelling removes any doubt concerning which works qualify for philosophical consideration and separate his aesthetics from that of Kantian formalism ruled by aesthetic ideas.

Schelling's discourses on *hearing* provide access both to art in its sense of Greek sacredness and to more general developments. These discourses constitute the opening part of chapter 4, under the heading "The Real Side of the Form of Art; or Formative Art." Section 76 reads: "*The indifference of the informing (Einbilden) of the infinite into the finite, taken purely as indifference, is* **sonority** *(Klang)*. *Or, with the informing (Einbilden) of the infinite into the finite, indifference as indifference can emerge only as sonority.*"[9]

On indifference: The notion of indifference, which clearly distinguishes Schelling's thought from Hegel's, reaches further toward radical otherness, that quasi-inaccessible source from which all appearances emerge. One finds movement toward this otherness insofar as opposition emerges from a region that can only be characterized negatively, as beyond darkness and light, or beyond reason and unreason—if indeed it makes any sense to speak of it as a region at all. In these terms *Geist* for Schelling is not "first of all," thought interpenetrates nature and art just as it makes itself manifest in all those operations deemed "higher."

Schelling distinguishes *Klang, Schall,* and *Laut* from one another; lexicographically, all three could be translated as "sound." Translator Douglas Stott renders them most ably as "sonority," "resonance," and "sound," respectively. This is another instance of Schelling's creative appropriation and transformation of Spinoza. Sonority (*Klang*) is to be thought as the analogue of Spinozist substance (e.g., as quantity). Resonance (*Schall*) is the analogical attribute of sonority. Sound (*Laut*), which Schelling characterizes as "interrupted resonance," is the analogical mode of that attribute. Sonority alone allows for the unity in the multiplicity to be discernible.

Stott's translation of *Einbilden* as "informing" is certainly correct. However *Bild*, the heart of the word, is rendered primarily as *image* when it occurs by itself. And as will be the case in Schelling's 1809 *Freiheitsschrift*, this same word *Einbilden* receives the strongest emphasis at the most critical point in the essay.

In terms of hearing, listen to the Hesiodic poem that begins "*ex archēs,*" from which Chaos first (*prōton*) came into being. Indifference in the Schellingian name for the *archē* is manifest only in its absence, that is, anterior to any "before" or "first." Consider also what is said of "sonority" in terms of its relation to magnetism in the philosophy of nature. Magnetism belongs to the particular body, thus is a *difference* of that body, hence magnetism is not pure. "[Sonority] is pure as such and is indifference only to the extent that it is separated from the body and is a form unto itself, as an absolute form. The latter is found only in sonority, for sonority is on the one hand living and active—in and for itself—and on the other hand a mere dimension in time, though not in space. . . . Sonority is resonance comprehended as continuity, as an uninterrupted flow of resonance."[10]

Can one not hear echoes of the Heraclitean *panta rhei* in Schelling's account of sonority? Can one not also hear perhaps more distant echoes of Parmenides's primordially undifferentiated Being in Schelling's thought of indifference? Can Schelling's presentation of undifferentiated differentiation be interpreted in terms of the Athenian Stranger's questioning of Parmenides in Plato's *Sophist*? The rumblings of these questions bear witness to the silent Greek depth driving the surface of Schelling's interpretation of Greek philosophy. In order for his doctrinal notion of the relation of infinite and finite in art to occur at all, the roiling archaic sounding beneath had to be taking place.

How may the surface content be characterized? Schelling's §77 reads: "The art form in which the real unity purely as such becomes potence and symbol is **music**." In §78–80, Schelling characterizes music as "the real unity becomes its own symbol," as "the particular *Einbilden* of unity into multiplicity," such that its "real unity—is rhythm," and most significantly, "rhythm in its completed state necessarily encompasses the other unity within itself, which is modulation" (trans. 110–111, 491–492, 142–143).

Once again Schelling invokes the ancients, declaring that they attributed the greatest aesthetic power to music. He also provides a noteworthy interpretation in the addendum to §79:

> Rhythm is the music within music, for the particularity of music is based precisely on its character as the informing of unity into a multiplicity. Since according to §79 rhythm is nothing more than this informing **within** music itself, it is thus the music within music, and, according to the nature of this art form, is the predominating feature within it.
>
> Only if we remember this proposition will we be able to comprehend scientifically particularly the contrast between ancient and modern music.[11]

This passage points to two key matters regarding the apprehension of music. First of all, the music within music—rhythm—is not *heard*, strictly speaking. More precisely, one must say phenomenologically that it is *felt* more than it is heard—or better, that the way of its apprehension dwells on the cusp between hearing and feeling and is reducible to neither. The access to rhythm, then, occurs concurrently with the hearing of modulated melody. At work beneath the surface of Schelling's discourse, providing the archaic primordial origin through which this discourse becomes possible, is the Heraclean *panta rhei*, normally rendered in English as "everything flows." The verb *rheō*, to flow, gives *rhuthmos* its sense.

There can be no doubt that rhythmical matters played a major role in the construction and transmission of the Homeric epics. Milman Parry's studies in *The Making of Homeric Verse* leave little for dispute on this matter.[12] Nevertheless, the epics cannot be primarily or even secondarily regarded as exercises in dactylic hexameter, nor can the Greek tragedies and comedies gain a genuine reception by means of rhythmic concerns alone. Parry's famous example of *epea pteroenta* provides a case in point. He contends that oral poetry depends upon an intricate and well-developed system of formulas, of which "on winged words" is one. It occurs often in the epics (124 times), and Homer employed it without regard to the meaning of these terms. His exhaustive study of its placement is convincing in one sense: it occurs only in certain lines where its meter is required to complete a report of what a figure happens to be saying. That is, there is no specificity to its employment.

Nevertheless, Parry's conclusion coheres with Schelling's much different analysis. The latter writes: "As little as we admittedly know about such [Greek] music, we do know that here, too, the realistic, plastic, heroic principle predominated, and it predominated solely by subordinating everything else to rhythm."[13] One experiences this and (conceding the point) other Homeric formulas not so much as elements *heard*, strictly speaking, or as residing at the cusp of hearing and feeling. This holds also for Parry's conclusion: "The Homeric student who [is aware of the formulas instead of 'looking for beauties where they are not'] will come back to the *Iliad* and the *Odyssey* better able to feel their conventional wording as the usual heroic language which ever sweeps ahead with force and fineness."[14]

Despite the enthusiasm for the relatively recent translations of Robert Fagles, the superiority of Richmond Lattimore's grayer translations of Homer's epics seems clear. Nevertheless, "winged words" has its own peculiar beauty even when experienced as conventional, namely, as an image of that aspect of the gift of logos by which we can speak to one another, just as it derives its place from its metrical placement, that is, its rhythm.

Schelling's theoretical treatments of melody and harmony inform his intriguing distinction between ancient and modern music. Of the three elements, Schelling will later call rhythm "the essence of the essence" because it finds itself always already present. Melody and harmony are subordinate, yet they are each themselves "the entire unity" because each encompasses the other from its own point of view. He calls melody "the absolute informing of the infinite into the finite."[15] Harmony is also the informing of the identity into difference, but in relation to the ideal unity that can expand into a second dimension and so bring voices of various kinds together. As a shorthand way of access to the difference, Schelling compares Sophocles to Shakespeare: "A work of Sophocles possesses pure rhythm, and only necessity is presented, it has no superfluous breadth; Shakespeare, on the other hand, is the greatest harmonist and the master of dramatic counterpoint; it is not the simple rhythm of a unique event but it simultaneously represents to us all that accompanies it and the reflex that comes from its various sides."[16]

Although there are occasions when Schelling seems to judge the art of his time in general to be superior to ancient music on account of the reflective Christian content that was unavailable to the ancients, his actual deed in the *Philosophy of Art*—which concerns itself the vast majority of the time with ancient matters in general—indicates another conclusion. Shakespeare's rapturous account of the fate of Lear's children spins out in a way "such that to each individual moment of the whole another moment is juxtaposed that both accompanies it and reflects it,"[17] suggesting that the modern divine poet surpasses his ancient colleagues. However, Schelling defends Greek music on account of its undeniably great strength even in the absence of harmonic elements, not to mention the vitality it has retained to his and to our day.

Therefore, one cannot conclude that Greek music has been *aufgehoben*, except *perhaps* in the sense that it is preserved. It has clearly neither been canceled nor overcome in such a way that it leads to a higher stage that leaves it behind. For Schelling, it cannot be *aufgehoben*, and not merely for theoretical (or practical) reasons. Rather, it carries with it the archaic fundament of his thought that he can no more shake off than he can shake off his own embodiment. It is his fate as a thinker not only to carry forth the gift of Greece in his thought but to live through this gift with his every step, even as he endeavors to surpass it with his "new" philosophy. One can feel its presence even in this Shakespeare interpretation, in which the expansion "beyond" rhythm into melody and harmony cannot be regarded as an extension beyond wholeness and, most of all, beyond necessity.

The meaning of *necessity* that now dominates philosophy bears witness to a developing evisceration of its sense. Necessity refers either to a logical inference of a certain kind, for example, given $(p \supset q)$ and p, q follows necessarily; it does not matter at all what p or q may represent, if indeed they represent anything at all. This is the basic sense of logical necessity. The other sense is tied to what we call efficient causality, which has its root in a problematic translation of Aristotle's *ek on*. The latter can be rendered literally as "that from which" or "out of which" something arises; Aristotle's examples are "the primary source of the change or coming to rest; e.g., the man who gave advice is a cause, the father is cause of the child, and generally what makes of what is made and what causes change of what is changed."[18]

Though the modern sense is certainly present in Aquinas and plays a major though subterranean role in Spinoza as shown above, the *locus classicus* for the necessity of truths that appear contingent since their opposites are not self-contradictory is Leibniz's principle of sufficient reason discussed in the opening section above, "in virtue of which we hold that there can be no fact real or existing, no statement true, unless there be a sufficient reason, why it should be so and not otherwise, although these reasons usually cannot be known by us."[19] If the chain of causes were open to our gaze, which it is not, we could discover these causes as they ultimately converge in the single originary substance. For Leibniz, efficient and final causes converge; goodness as well as necessity constitute the universe. This is why I consider Spinoza the thinker who is in strong touch with the ancient dark undercurrents that inform modern philosophy and make it possible. Leibniz is surely a great thinker, but he is a thinker for whom these same dark currents proved too terrible in all their power. The final causality that Spinoza so despised is Leibniz's recourse to what I contend is modern philosophy's concealment of the dark source from which it arises, a concealment that takes place in its other great thinkers from both sides of the rationalist/empiricist divide.

Within the ancient notion of necessity, we find certain slippages that provide a clue to its vital instinctive sense. In Homer it occurs in situations where the figures are constrained or compelled to act in a certain manner.[20] In Parmenides strong necessity held Being within its limits. The so-called ambiguity in Parmenides between the "is" of existence and the "is" of predication could not be farther from his thought. In the myth of Er in Book X of Plato's *Republic*, Necessity names an unbreakable bond. In Timaeus's logos of the second beginning, necessity "sets things adrift." What could these three "have in common?" Schelling's thought, insofar as it draws from a genuinely Greek source, exhibits a way to regard their unity.

The unity of Greek thought expresses itself primarily as a *living* unity, that is, it cannot be reducible to concepts, or to facts, or to feelings but—to say it in modern terms—it is made manifest in all three simultaneously. In other words, if we were to characterize this unity with a single notion, it is a *poetically experienced* unity. Necessity is strong: it cannot be escaped or overcome. The Spindle of Necessity grants a choice of souls in Hades: this choice, once made, seals the next life for a human being. The necessity that sets things adrift must withdraw without showing its own face in order that things may come into being and show themselves.

At the close of this section on philosophy of art, we should remind ourselves of the emphasized passage from philosophy of nature, where Schelling wrote "*even unconditioned necessity becomes freedom once more.*" The interpretation of this phrase will prove to be crucial in the section on the *Freiheitsschrift*, which will follow the brief comments on the 1802 lecture series (translated as *On University Studies*).

Lectures concerning the Method of Academic Studies (1803)

The German title is *Vorlesungen über die Methode des akademischen Studiums*. The imprecise but often useful translation bears the title *On University Studies*.[21] Although the nature of the audience for these lectures is unclear, its size was apparently quite large. Schelling already enjoyed a glowing reputation at age twenty-seven, and many of the philosophical convictions that inform the *Philosophy of Art* are also found here. However, they are presented much more broadly, and in a way that suggests a beginning class and/or a class including people unfamiliar with philosophy. *On University Studies* discussed here shares the same spirit regardless of subject matter, namely, the demand that the various disciplines be undertaken in terms of what Schelling repeatedly calls the idea (*Idee*). Ideal and real, at odds in the finite realm, unite in the infinite. Philosophy's task, as the science of all sciences, consists of orienting the human mind toward this ultimate unity of which particulars are the mere afterimages. In fact, all particularity implies universality, as only philosophy can demonstrate.

The lecture series frequently returns to gestures that point to access of at least certain nonrational human talents. For example, "the philologist stands with the artist on the highest level—or rather, both interpenetrate in him" (III, V, 246).[22] In an oblique criticism of Kant, he writes: "Morality is a godlike disposition, elevation above determination through the concrete into the realm of the absolutely (*schlechthin*) universal" (III, V, 276). The role of art is frequently marked, most provocatively in Schelling's account of "the historian's art," which should be studied methodically as "the greatest and most astonishing (*erstaunenswürdigen*) drama" (III, V, 310), and "as a kind of epic that has no definite beginning and no definite end" (III, V, 311).

One can hardly deny the powerful Greek echoes here as well. The science of philology, like all of the highest sciences, requires *inspiration* as well as intellectual intuition. The study of the epics and the tragedies requires that one rise above technical knowledge in order to behold their lofty origin in the ideas. One can also hardly avoid thinking of the image of Socrates who, governed by his bond to Apollo and to the *daimonion* that restrained him from inappropriate action, functioned in his world without need of recourse to a law. The interpretation of history as epic drama surely signals a retrieval of the poetic sense that powered the Greek experience of life for Schelling.

However, these heights could not be heights if their echoes did not emerge from the darkest depths, from Hesiod's Chaos, from the Hades of Heraclitus and Plato. What one finds as its analogue in both the philosophy of art and the philosophy of nature, namely, *indifference*, is nowhere mentioned in these lectures. In the preceding works, indifference presented itself as a null point out of which both ideal and real took their equally originary departure. In this popularized and/or introductory presentation of Schelling's thought, perhaps it had no place. As we move forward into the *Freiheitsschrift*, the thought—if it is indeed a thought—of indifference moves into its *positive* sense.

From a more significant viewpoint, the *Lectures* display the same struggle that was foreshadowed in the earlier texts, namely, the dual claims of the superiority of the Christian viewpoint and the more vibrant claims of the ancient Greek experience.

> With Christianity the relation between the nature and the ideal world had to be reversed, just as in paganism nature was the manifest (*das Offenbare*) while the ideal world withdrew, in Christianity the ideal world became manifest and nature withdrew as secret (*Geheimnis*). In Christianity the ideal world was progressively revealed while nature receded into the background. To the Greeks nature as such was immediate and divine in itself, because at the same time their gods were not supernatural or extranatural. The modern world was closed off to them because they did not conceive it in itself, but rather as allegory of the invisible and spiritual world. (III, V, 289; my translation)

Accordingly, the idea of God become human is the end (*Ende*) of the idea of the ancient world of gods, and the reversal is complete insofar as the incarnate God assumes the humblest rather than the highest and strongest position.

However, as if in conflict with himself, Schelling's deed clashes with the latter claim. The lectures conclude with a return to the world of the Greeks: "Even though the public at large may find it hard to grasp that art is a necessary, integral part of a state founded on ideas, we should at least recollect the ancient world, when festivals, public monuments, dramatic performances, and other actions of public life were only different branches of One universal, objective, and living work of art" (III, V, 352). The "new race" posited earlier can only appear in this light as both Christian and Greek, but at the same time and in the same way neither Christian nor Greek. Christianity closed off the ancient world that is required for life. The ancient world throbs eternally beneath the modern world as the former's dark source. The infinite and the finite shatter against the wall of sense, delivering the new race over to madness.

The *Freiheitsschrift* (1809)

Given its full title, *Philosophische Untersuchungen über das Wesen der menschlichen Freiheit und die damit zusammenhängenden Gegenstände* (Concerning the Essence of Human Freedom and the Objects Connected with It), one can surely understand why Hegel regarded this work as a new development, entirely separate from what preceded it as well as "deep and speculative."[23] It does not present a system. Nor does it seem to draw much upon the earlier writings. The issue of human freedom seems to arise from nowhere, as does Schelling's treatment of it. The *Freiheitsschrift* is his first published work in several years and is his final publication. The issue of freedom versus necessity did not occur in this manner in any of the earlier writings. Insofar as it pertains to the theme of probing into philosophy's dark sources, this issue did not trouble the Greeks or exist for them at all.

Schelling places this issue in all of its sharpness in the early pages of the *Freiheitsschrift*: "For this great task alone is the unconscious and invisible mainspring of all striving after knowledge, from the lowest to the highest; without the contradiction (*Widerspruch*) of freedom and necessity not only philosophy, but every higher willing of the spirit would sink to the death which is peculiar to those sciences in which this contradiction has no application" (IV, VII, 338). Here, necessity (the necessity of the whole) and freedom are called *contradictory*. However, the contradiction is necessary for living science, and serves as the concealed inspiration without which life could not first come forth.

Where in the life of ancient Greece do we find what I will clumsily call an analogue to the contradiction of freedom and necessity? Contradiction! It seems before Plato nothing like contradiction was recorded,[24] and not until Aristotle was it formalized.[25] However, Schelling's thought finds itself always already informed by Greek poetry, in relation to which formal logic is at most a second-order phenomenon if not a phenomenon even more distant from life. For Schelling, the struggle (*Widerstreit*) makes itself manifest in the contradiction (*Widerspruch*) out of which all higher strivings and indeed all life emerges. *Spruch* translates the Greek *logos*. Schelling's sense of logos and its indistinguishability from mythos will soon prove to be a crucial theme in the *Freiheitsschrift*. Once again, Hesiod provides indirect access.

As the *Theogony* sings, the race of gods came into being by means of the rape of Gaia (Earth) by Ouranos (Heaven), begetting twelve Titans (Oceanus, Coeus, Crius, Hyperion, Iapetos, Theia, Rhea, Themis, Mnemosyne, Phoebe, Tethys, and Cronus; also three Cyclopes: Brontes, Steropes, and Arges, and three Hecatoncheires, Kottos, Briareos, and Gyges). Ouranos feared and despised the three Cyclopes, and consigned them to Tartarus, where he did not have to contend with their strength; he did the same with the hideous and mighty hundred-headed Hecatoncheires, who were overwhelmingly powerful, far more powerful than their father. However, mother's love prevailed (at least somewhat), as

Gaia appealed to the Titans to release her imprisoned children. Cronus alone agreed, castrating his father with a sickle. A particularly salient outcome of the castration occurred as a result of Cronus's casting the testicles of his father out to sea, where they foamed and took shape as the goddess Aphrodite.

What has any of this to do with the *Freiheitsschrift*? Recall that one aspect of Schelling's unique contribution concerns the philosophy of nature—more precisely, that nature be experienced as a *first-order phenomenon of life* rather than at a distance and under a kind of sterile empirical observation. In this sense, the Greek figures are not "personifications" of natural events. Rather, the so-called natural events are the Greek figures with their vicarious truth subtracted. The Cyclopes are first of all Brontes, Steropes, and Arges; only secondarily are they "thunder," "lightning," and "brightness." This vicarious truth will prove to be especially important toward the end of the *Freiheitsschrift*, when the relation of system to life manifests itself in the most profound manner.

Consider the generation and the interplay of the Greek gods. The origin? Rape. The first father threw his children down into Tartarus. Why? They were more powerful than him. Motherly love gained the Titans' release. How? By castration of her husband. And the blood from the castration? The blood found its way to the sea foam, where Aphrodite was born. How? "Parthenogenesis" is quite inaccurate and inappropriate. There was no *parthenos* (virgin). The birth is utterly unaccountable, and one can locate nothing in her faux parentage that could account for her beauty that shines brightest of all.

When Schelling thinks "freedom," "necessity," and their "contradiction," one can hear the procession of and the turmoil in the generation of the Greek gods. In Schelling, Kant's third antinomy occurs as flesh and blood, as life-giving *agon*. In the *Freiheitsschrift*, the three Kantian critiques are not merely united in his effort to present a living system, but further they become something analogous to a dramatic backdrop for an unprecedented poetic/philosophical act. At once logos and mythos, arguments metamorphose into tales and tales transform into arguments. The logic of Schelling requires that one follow these transformations in a manner that *lets them be transformations*, that is, lets them show the originary order/disorder that constitutes them in every case and as a whole. To say the same thing another way, Schelling's language makes itself manifest at once as both poetic logic and logical poetry.

The first sentence of the *Freiheitsschrift* points to its peculiar way of layering, in which conceptualization constitutes only one element: "Philosophical investigations concerning the essence of human freedom can in part concern the right concept of freedom, for although the feeling of freedom is immediately stamped in each, the fact of freedom lies in no way so near to the surface that merely to express it in words would not require a more than usual purity and depth of sense; in part the investigations can concern the connection (*Zusammenhang*) of this concept with the whole of a scientific (*wissenschaftlichen*) worldview" (IV, VII, 336).

The threefold of concept, feeling, and fact can be seen as Schelling's appropriation of Kant's division into theoretical, aesthetic, and practical regions with the practical enjoying primacy. However, the genitive of "the whole of a scientific worldview" can be read both objectively and subjectively. That is, the phrase could be read as saying that the scientific worldview in question is a view from the standpoint of the whole; and it could be read saying that the whole emerges from the standpoint of a certain scientific worldview.

Schelling's modifying article, "*a* scientific worldview," strongly suggests that there may be other such worldviews. Also in the first paragraph, he says of freedom that it "must be one of the dominant centers (*Mittelpunkte*) of the system" (IV, 228, 336). Necessity, clearly, must be the other. Thus, the contradiction makes the system animate, that is, the contradiction that makes the system *alive* at its origin, must somehow occur as *bicentral*. But bicentrality—what sense could this have?

"Bicentrality" cannot be found in any American dictionary or in the *Oxford English Dictionary*—nor is there a German word in Schelling that would characterize this situation toward which Schelling's discourse inexorably leads. However, Schelling's recourse to an ancient text—or more precisely, an ancient text reflecting upon other, more ancient texts—provides a window to Schelling's notion of system and science, while at the same time directing the discourse toward a twofold still more originary than any heretofore treated. In *Against the Grammarians*, Sextus Empiricus influences Schelling in the following: "But whoever would take the departure from physical theory would know, that an entirely ancient doctrine that like is known by like (which presumably came from Pythagoras, though Plato also hit upon it, and was much earlier expressed by Empedocles), will understand that the philosopher can maintain such (divine) knowledge because he alone preserves his understanding pure and undarkened by evil, can conceive the god outside him with the god in him" (IV, VII, 337).[26]

This passage serves for Schelling as a rejoinder to those who would offer several objections: (1) that the notions of freedom and system are inconsistent; (2) that the two notions are contradictory in general and in themselves (*an sich*); and (3) that human understanding could never succeed in attaining that insight. Such a response clearly resides beyond anything belonging to any other aspect of the movement known as German Idealism. Empedocles famously declared himself to be a deathless god, and Sextus defends him against the charges of boastfulness (*huperopsian*) and contempt (*anephthegchthai*) for all others.[27] This citation should be seen not only as a defense of Empedocles but also and even primarily as an illumination of Schelling's own procedure. It is a further clarification of what Schelling called "intellectual intuition," and "inspiration." As an heir to Kant, one can hardly imagine a more daring philosophical procedure than this recourse to Empedocles through Sextus.

Among other incapacities of the grammarians is the ability "to follow Plato when he says 'Between the Being that is indivisible and remains always the same and the Being that is divisible in bodies, he blended a third form of Being compounded of the two, that is to say, out of the Same and the other,' and the rest of the context, about which all of the interpreters of Plato keep silence."[28] Strictly speaking, it is incorrect to claim that Plato interpreters are silent about the *chora* as it occurs in the *Timaeus*. Sextus surely knew that Aristotle offered a discussion of *chora*. However, this discussion could not have missed the mark more. John Sallis details the gross textual error:

> Yet the passage [identifying the *chora* with primary matter] that is, at once, both most decisive and most puzzling occurs in Book 4 of the *Physics*: "This is why Plato says in the *Timaeus* that matter and the *chora* are the same; for the receptive and the *chora* are one and the same . . . he declares that place [*topos*] and the *chora* are the same" (209b).
>
> One cannot but be struck by the lack of correspondence between this passage and the text of the *Timaeus*.[29]

Thinking now through the claim of Sextus concerning the silence of the Plato interpreters on the *chora*, at the very least Aristotle did not *hear* the logos of the *Timaeus*. Sallis spoke of it as "decisive" and "puzzling." I shall call it *noise*, a warped mimesis of silence, its privation. This is not to say that Schelling surpasses the limits of knowledge as these are inscribed in the Kantian critiques. Rather, a certain expansion is sounded that is already implicit in Kant. On one side, the Paralogisms disclose the limits of the "I think." This proposition is transcendentally ideal and empirically real. It extends no farther than the appearances to inner sense. There is no known self in itself, and no proof of the soul's immortality in a theoretical sense. There is, however, a *thinkable* self, even a thinkable immortal soul.

We return, therefore, to the aforementioned notion of bicentrality that includes both what I will call an epistemological Kantian narrative in which the tension between freedom and necessity constitutes the contradiction that animates all true philosophy, and the glimpsed unclouded unity in which divine knowing consists of intellectual intuition, that is, intuition that creates its object in the very act of thinking it. Taking this together, the philosopher's calling involves a most peculiar purification: one must somehow keep darkness from entering one's understanding—and/or dismiss darkness from it—so that with such an understanding one can grasp the external god through the internal god. The external god, however, cannot merely be conceived as an image of the unity of appearances under transcendental apperception and the categories. It must also, and perhaps especially, conceive the *chora*—that is, conceive that which escapes conceptualization. What can be said, then, concerning the language of divine knowing? This language speaks of matters that are so bright as to exceed the measure of human apprehension. The bicentrality of thought mirrors the duplicity of language: language occurs rationally and mythically at once. This is the language of the philosopher, not the language of the poet. The latter sings the darkness out of which all things emerged. The former sings the light that shines on all things that are beheld.

In Schelling's discussion of the copula, we gain a sense of the essential undercurrent of linguistic bicentrality. He recalls "the profound Ancient logic," in which the "is" that unites the subject and the predicate of a judgment does not at all signify a tautological relationship between them, nor is the same thing thought in both subject and predicate even when they appear to be the same, as in "a body is a body." Strangely, Schelling identifies the aforementioned ancient sense by the Latin *"an-*

tecedens et consequens" and later by "*impicitum et explicitum*" (IV, 234, 342). The "et," that is, the "and" may be heard as the gathering of the "is." "Gathering," I strongly suggest, can be heard as the Schellingian image of bicentrality. In his creative appropriation of Leibniz, Schelling also gathers the law of identity and the law of sufficient reason into one, saying that the latter law is precisely as originary (*ein ebenso ursprüngliches*) (IV, VII, 346) as the law of identity.

In §31 and §32 of the *Monadology*, Leibniz differentiates between the highest principles:

> Our reasoning is based upon *two great principles*: first, *that of contradiction*, by means of which we decide that to be *false* which involves contradiction and that to be *true* which contradicts or is opposed to the false. And second, the *principle of sufficient reason*, in virtue of which we believe that no fact can be real or existing and no statement true unless it has a sufficient reason why it should be thus and not otherwise. Most frequently, however, these reasons cannot be known by us.[30]

Schellingian bicentrality brings them together. Though it may seem at first that Schelling collapses the contingent truths to which the principle of sufficient reason applies to the necessary truths to which the law of contradiction applies, one can creatively transform the Leibnizian twofold while retaining its integrity. In the *Discourse on Metaphysics* Leibniz opens the way to what will seem like Schellingian excess, namely, his declaration that *all* propositions are in essence a priori, despite the opacity of sufficient reason to us.

From a human perspective, any point in Alexander the Great's life may be presented in a contingent proposition and must be learned through history. "God, however, seeing the individual concept, or hæcceity, of Alexander, sees in it at the same time the foundation and the reason of all the predicates that can be truly stated of him,"[31] such that every moment is full of his entire past and entire future under the gaze of eternity. With such a view, it appears that for Leibniz all propositions are ultimately analytic.

Can the same be said for Schelling? The answer to this is either "clearly no," or "only with much qualification." Logos for Schelling does not have the sense of "argument" or "proposition." As I attempted to demonstrate in *Schelling's Dialogical Freedom Essay*, Schelling's language crosses rational and mythical speech. The "*-spruch*" in *Widerspruch* returns logos to its anterior tie to mythos. Its most suitable analogue is *logismō nothō*, bastard logos, named in Plato's *Timaeus* as appropriate for speaking of the *chora*. Schelling's earlier works, as we have seen, arrived at an unground or indifference point out of which all dualities take their departure. The *Freiheitsschrift* finally effects the ultimate transformation of indifference.

With this, another and deeper—or perhaps more lively—presence of Heraclitus can be discerned sounding and breathing below Schelling's text than can be distinguished below Spinoza's once again: "Listening not to me but to the *logos*, it is wise to agree that all being is one (*ouk emou alla tou logou akousantas homologein sophon estin hen panta einai*)."[32] In Spinoza, this undertone sounded a fundamental oneness governing all things, however contrary or even contradictory. In Schelling, this distinct and distinguishable ongoing susurration takes its departure not from a primordial oneness, but from what might well be called a primordial none-ness, or from what Schelling will later call a neither-nor.

Schelling's Spinoza critique aims at the latter's positing the constituents of God as *things*, and not at all at his pantheism. One must listen, then, with a nuanced attention. "The procession of things from God is a self-revelation of God. But God can only become manifest in that which is similar to, in free beings (*Wesen*) who act from themselves, for whose being (*Sein*) there is no ground but God, but who are as God is. He speaks, and they are there" (IV, VII, 347). For what—or for whom—are we listening? We listen for the articulate word as the sole mark of freedom. In order for this word to be articulate, it must be composed of vowels and consonants. "For the eternal spirit speaks out the unity or the word in nature. The expressed (real) word however, is only in the unity of light and darkness (vowel and consonant)" (IV, 255, 363).

Thus, without the principle of darkness as fully present in human beings, God cannot manifest himself. With this, we once again experience Hesiod's Chaos out of which the cosmos emerges in the bloodiest and most violent manner. Schelling has said that paganism and Christianity are equally originary (*gleichursprünglish*). Bicentrality reiterates itself in the equal-originariness of paganism and Christianity. With respect to knowledge, both hover in the space between reason and inspiration. The language of Schelling, once again, is mythical.

With this is mind, let us examine what the names reveal. Of course, there neither were nor could be any "pagan" synagogues, churches, or institutions. Paganism in general referred to local, usually rustic polytheistic religions, and took its meaning in terms of its difference from Abrahamic monotheistic religions. In addition to the nonexistence of any declared "pagans" (excepting contemporary Wiccans and the like), the term carried a pejorative connotation. In order to enter into the full force of his thought, it must be borne in mind that this is not only emphatically the case for Schelling, but that their equal status fuels his thought in a unique manner. Nietzsche will abandon Christian imagery and a Christian component from his thought altogether, though the power of the Greek gods will prove similarly decisive. In Schelling alone do we find these two primary and dominant religious traditions interacting and clashing creatively.

Thus, Judeo-Christianity gives "paganism" its name. However, in Schelling's thought, paganism—at least in the sense of the Greek Olympian and Chthonic gods—always responds. I should say: "paganism" has always already responded because of the nature of Schelling's language. Schelling has likened Spinoza's pantheism to the rigid statue of Pygmalion carved by the king that came alive only after the attentions of Aphrodite. In Schelling's words, it would come to life if it could receive a soul through the warm breath of love.[33] Absent this, "it could readily be compared to the oldest images of the godheads in that the fewer individually living features issuing from them the more secret-bearing [or oracular] they appeared" (IV, VII, 350). In either case, Schelling's discourse echoes the ancient intercourse of Spinozism that is not present in the Kantian overtones of his (Schelling's) thought.

It is clear that the language of both Christianity and "paganism' takes place in terms of their *imagery*, that is, not in terms of any claims of knowledge of or access to originals. Similarly, Schelling's most often noted and most fundamental duplicity of God as ground and God as existence and the ground of God's existence takes place as the primordial play of images—that is, the play of images anterior to which one can neither go nor imagine. Accordingly, one can call the collection of qualities belonging to the side of existence—Understanding, Unity, Form, Order, Rule, God himself, God's reflexive representation—"Christian." On the side of ground, one can call its collection of qualities—will, longing, unruly, darkness, Plato's "matter"—"pagan," or more specifically, ancient Greek imagery.

I see no defensible claim that Spinoza's God can be thought as religious or transcendent in any sense. It makes no difference here whether he is called an atheist, a pantheist (as Schelling calls him), or a panentheist. Schelling claims that Spinoza's system needs "the warm breath of love." What does he mean? At this point, the Christian mythos of *agapē* meets the Greek mythos of eros. The latter deprives human beings of their good sense but, in a philosophical sense, inspires that divine madness out of which prophesy, healing, and great art spring—also that love peculiar to philosophers that is both overwhelmingly passionate and utterly temperate. Bicentrality shows itself once again in the collision of the two ways of mythos that has always already taken place. It redounds to Schelling's credit that his thought embraces Greek eros as equipollent with Christian *agapé*. While several texts can be found among Schelling's *Freedom Essay* that appear to "favor" the Christian mythos, both their context and their absence at the end of the essay demonstrate the ever-abiding presence of the dark principle.

The birth of nature and the birth of history repeat bicentrality and the abiding pervasiveness of the dark principle. "The birth of spirit is the realm of history, as the birth of light is the realm of nature. The same periods of creation found in the latter are also in the former, and the one is the likeness and the explanation of the other" (IV, VII, 377–378). While the birth of nature is "first," both follow directly from what Schelling calls the eternal essence of God out of his ground. Nature occurs as inarticulate, yet resides silently as if shimmering in the human unconscious. God's need to reveal himself requires a living ground that is independent of him. In nontheological nonmythical language, rule, form, and order require unruliness, formlessness and disorder; understanding requires blindness. In terms of the treatise's title, good requires evil.

Concerning *freedom*, there is no word for it—for its analogue—in Greek. Like the gods who inhabit Greek life, no proof of their existence is offered since none is required; that is how intimately present they are. The so-called problem of freedom intertwines only with the advent of an all-powerful and all good transcendent God. Augustine's *On the Freedom of the Will* is the *locus classicus* of the traditional view that reconciles the presence of evil together with that of a perfect and omniscient God. It does so by regarding evil as *un*real, as the privation of being.

Schelling's thought, once again to its supreme credit, rejects such a view and recognizes that the so-called problem of evil cannot be met except by affirming both the reality and the nature of evil. Far from evil's exhibition—or nonexhibition—as mere privation, evil provokes horror and loathing in us.

From what does evil emerge? From the "elements," distinguishable only after the event of creation: God himself, the ground of God's existence that is in him but differentiated from him, and freedom. What, then, is freedom? Schelling calls it the "power" or "potentiality" (*Vermögen*) for good and evil. The word *Vermögen* sets off the human domain from the divine domain, both of which are indicated in mythical language. In God, freedom and necessity are fused—God can only be good. "Vermögen" in this context implies not only power but also "potentiality." Given the Spinozist conception of God with which Schelling works, all is actual.

In human freedom, freedom and necessity are separable in the following manner: the human being is necessarily bound to good *and evil*. The account of the dark principle both images and accounts for the power of good and evil in humanity. This view seems to echo Kant's in *Religion and the Limits of Reason Alone*, in that no neutral region between them finds recognition. The account of creation may be seen as an image of human freedom. Human freedom is nothing in the way of an attribute, nothing but a potentiality that itself requires an external provocation (solicitation) in order to awaken at all. Human freedom awakens nothing other than the twofoldness of principles that already dwell in the human being. Just as the ground is neither good nor evil, the free human being is neither good nor evil. This is the reiteration of the notion of bicentrality in human beings. The human manifestation of it is called *spirit*, in which the selfhood of humanity makes light its own in the midst of evil.

Bicentrality echoes with particular force in the births of nature and of history—the "and" binds them into a heterogeneous unity. "The birth of spirit is the realm of history, as the birth of light is the realm of nature. The same stages of creation which exist in the latter are also in the former; and the one is the symbol and explanation of the other. . . . For evil is, of course, nothing other than the primal basis of existence insofar as it strives toward actualization in created beings, and thus it is in fact only the higher potency of the basis operating in nature" (IV, VII, 378).

Following this, Schelling gives a mythical account of the gradual unfolding of both nature and history that roughly coheres with the account of the various ages of humanity discussed above. Setting this account back into the archaic framework operative in the Hesiodic mythos that has underpinned this exegesis thus far, Schelling declares an age before consciousness of good and evil, that is, an age of innocence, and goes so far as to suggest that "the primal ground of nature perhaps had attempted a creation when the divine powers in him operated alone before" (IV, VII, 378), the divine forces remained concealed within it; the basis "may have itself attempted a creation," but slipped back into chaos since the word of love was lacking. Yet another peculiar image of bicentrality occurs: in the gradual unfolding of creation, "God himself moved only in accordance with his nature and not in accordance with his heart" (IV, VII, 378). The progressive unfolding made itself manifest originally in a golden age of indifference free of good and evil, followed by "an age of sovereign gods and heroes, or the omnipotence of nature, in which the basis showed what it was capable of in itself."[34] Then followed the aforementioned age of indifference, which culminated in its acme with the visible beauty of the gods of ancient Greece.

This marks the limit of what the basis can accomplish by itself—the basis cannot beget a creative unity. Schelling posits a consequent disease that returns all things to chaos (the Dark Ages, perhaps) once again. A second division of forces begins, in which out of an original concealment in the depths the spirit of evil emerges and the spirit of good emerges to do battle with it everywhere. Where at first signs and portents to individual men signal the eternal struggle, eventually the word sounds forth and is articulated as the center that will contend with every challenge from its opponent. However, chaos can never be overcome or canceled out. Without the ever-churning unruly basis, nothing can be fashioned except insofar is it already contains within itself form and order in latency.

In the ultimate sense there is no "before and after," no "first this, then that," all is *sub specie aeternitatis* to use Spinoza's term. Schelling's idiosyncratic notion of indifference creatively transforms this thought, binding it to the swirling formless chaos anterior to all birth of which Hesiod sang. Recall that Earth came "next," "followed by" Eros, who unsettled the good sense of human beings. Schellingian eros unifies the Greek notion that addresses its tempestuous sense and its Christian sense of *philia* in which its selfless sense predominates. Perhaps the

Platonic notion that addresses its kinship with measure in divine madness already unites them in a way, but for Schelling, system requires that all-benevolence must reign as one of its centers.

Thus, the contradiction of freedom and necessity that is necessary for living philosophy shows itself to unfold out of the anterior Greek chaos that undergirds it—and undergirds all modern philosophy.

Notes

1. F. W. J. Schelling, *Schellings Werke*, vol. 1, *Jugendschriften 1793–1798* (Munich: C. H. Beck, 1965). All translations mine.
2. Note: the first Roman numeral refers to the volume number; the second to the location within the volume of the particular work cited; the concluding Arabic numeral refers to the actual page number of the work.
3. An Aeschylus scholar named Schüz and the editor of the volume in which Schelling's essay appeared offered the view that Prometheus was an actual person.
4. F. W. J. Schelling, *First Outline of a System of the Philosophy of Nature*, trans. Keith Peterson (Albany: State University of New York Press, 2004), 201.
5. Note: "trans" refers to the page number of Peterson's translation. The two Roman numerals, followed by the Arabic numeral, refer respectively to the volume number of Schelling's *Werke*, the location of the work within that volume, and the actual page number, respectively.
6. Parmenides, in G. S. Kirk, J. E. Raven, and M. Schofield, *The Presocratic Philosophers* (Cambridge: Cambridge University Press, 1983), Frag. 298, 251.
7. Hesiod, *Works and Days*, in *Theogony, Works and Days, Testamonia*, trans. Glenn W. Most (Cambridge, MA: Harvard University Press, 2007), lines 180–200.
8. This passage occurs *before* the German text begins: F. W. J. Schelling, *Philosophy of Art*, trans. Douglas Stott (Minneapolis: University of Minnesota Press, 1989), 4. Since Schelling's texts often appear in different places, I have used this translation as my point of reference for this section.
9. Ibid., trans. 107.
10. Ibid., trans. 108.
11. Ibid., trans. 111.
12. Milman Parry, *The Making of Homeric Verse* (Oxford: Oxford University Press, 1971).
13. Schelling, *Philosophy of Art*, trans. 113.
14. Parry, *The Making of Homeric Verse*, 418.
15. Schelling, *Philosophy of Art*, trans. 113.
16. Ibid., 115. My emendation of the German.
17. Ibid., 117.
18. Aristotle, *Physics*, in *The Basic Works of Aristotle*, ed. Richard McKeon, trans. W. D. Ross (New York: Random House, 1970), 241.

19. Gottfried Wilhelm Leibniz, *Monadology*, in *Discourse on Metaphysics and Other Essays*, trans. Daniel Garber and Roger Arieu (Indianapolis: Hackett, 1991).

20. For an excellent list of such occurrences in the epics, see Richard John Cunliffe, *A Lexicon of the Homeric Dialect* (Norman: University of Oklahoma Press, 1963), 31.

21. F. W. J. Schelling, *On University Studies*, ed. N. Guterman, trans. E. S. Morgan (Athens: Ohio University Press), 1966.

22. All quotations from Schelling's 1802 *Lectures on University Studies* are mine.

23. Georg Wilhelm Friedric Hegel, *Vorlesungen über die Geschichte der Philosophie, Band III* (Leipzig: Phillip Reklam, 1971), 619.

24. See Plato, *Republic*, Book IV, 463.

25. Aristotle, *Metaphysics*, 1011b13–14.

26. In Sextus Empiricus, *Against the Professors*, trans. R. G. Bury (Cambridge, MA: Harvard University Press, 1949), 177.

27. Ibid., 179.

28. Ibid., 175.

29. John Sallis, *Chorology: On Beginnings in Plato's Timaeus* (Bloomington: Indiana University Press, 1999), 152.

30. Leibniz, *Monadology*, 72.

31. Leibniz, *Discourse on Metaphysics*, §8, 8.

32. Heraclitus, in Kirk, Raven, and Schofield, *Presocratic Philosophers*, Frag. 196, 187.

33. See Ovid, *Metamorphoses*, trans. Frank Justus Miller (Cambridge, MA: Harvard University Press, 1984), 10, 243–246.

34. Ibid., 56 (IV, 271, 379).

Coda
Nietzsche as Crux

THE PRIMARY SIGNIFICANCE of *The Birth of Tragedy out of the Spirit of Music* in terms of modern philosophy concerns the way it lays out its concealed anteriority, the life-giving darkness that resides beneath its surface giving it what life it has. Only Kant and Schopenhauer among modern philosophers receive explicit praise. Kant earns his by limiting the power of reason and of therefore achieving the victory over optimism hidden in the essence of logic; Schopenhauer earns his by sharing in this victory and by interpreting the "real" world as comprised of dream images, and the awe that results from an event that suddenly violates the principle of sufficient reason.

The "Attempt at a Self-Criticism" serves as the aforementioned crux. Written in 1886, some fourteen years after the original text was published, Nietzsche pulled back from this earlier praise, writing:

> How I regret now that in those days I lacked the courage (or immodesty?) to permit myself in every way an individual language of my own for such individual views and hazards—and that instead I tried laboriously to express by means of Schopenhauerian and Kantian formulas strange and new valuations which were basically at odds with Kant's and Schopenhauer's spirit and taste! What, after all, did Schopenhauer think of tragedy?

> "That which bestows on everything tragic its peculiar elevating force"—he says in *The World as Will and Representation*—"is the discovery that the world, that life, can never give real satisfaction and hence is *not worthy* of our affection: this constitutes the tragic spirit—it leads to resignation."

> How differently Dionysus spoke to me! How far removed I was from all this resignationism. But there is something far worse in this book, something I now regret still than that I obscured and spoiled Dionysian premonitions with Schopenhauerian formulations: namely, that

> I *spoiled* the grandiose *Greek problem*, as it had arisen before my eyes . . . , by introducing the most modern problems.[1]

However, these apparently self-denigrating statements mark the epoch-making transformation that Nietzsche enacts for both modern philosophy and its liberated aftermath. After working through the tradition and wringing out of it whatever it could yield in service to his nascent vision, he abandons those elements that would falsify it. Among them, Nietzsche gives special mention to one in particular that receives no mention in the original text, namely, "the careful and hostile silence with which Christianity is treated throughout the whole book."[2] Hostile to life, measuring the amoral character of life in accord with a standard not only alien to it but diametrically and perversely opposed to it, Nietzsche declaims ceremoniously: "It was against morality that my instinct turned with this questionable book, long ago; it was an instinct that aligned itself with life and that discovered for itself a fundamentally opposite doctrine and valuation of life—purely artistic and anti-Christian. What to call it? As a philologist and man of words I baptized it, not without taking some liberty—for who could claim to know the rightful name of the Antichrist?—in the name of a Greek god: I called it Dionysian."[3]

What, in light of the above, can be said concerning Spinoza and Schelling? They are the thinkers who were most directly stirred by the phenomenon called the Dionysian by Nietzsche. Their thought was surely bound to a notion of God: Schelling's was bound specifically to the Christian God, Spinoza's to a rational God, and Nietzsche's was bound to the Greek demigod Dionysus. However, all three had ears that empowered them to think against the tradition within which they found themselves having to work.

From the outset of *The Birth of Tragedy*, reason finds itself every bit as excluded as the Christian God. One might say that Nietzschean hostility extends back through the entirety of the Western tradition, stopping to praise only those thinkers who sought to limit reason's influence. In its place—or to speak more precisely, from the outset of human activity once the mask provided by reason is ripped away—are instincts (*Triebe*). The Apollonian impulse drives toward clarity, rule, form, and order; that is to say, it drives toward individuation. The Dionysian impulse drives toward chaos, drunkenness, dismemberment. That is to say, it drives toward return to originary nature as its first home. The two impulses are normally at odds, antagonistic to one another. There is no God and/or no reason to effect a compromise or reconciliation. The two do not together make a dualism on account of their resistance to assimilation of any kind. Rather, they constitute a duplicity (*Duplizität*). Where Schelling's boldness consisted in his ascribing a dark basis by virtue of which God could give birth to himself, there remained the residue of what Heidegger would call (perhaps too quickly) ontotheology. Schelling still held onto the notion of unity, even if this notion had to be achieved and had to emerge out of primal indifference. For Nietzsche the only manifestation that could merit being called a unity is an artwork, and such unity can only occur under conditions that could best be described as *magical*. It is a unity born of struggle and contradiction but merging somehow in an unwilled yet powerful reconciliation in Greek tragedy.

Although Nietzsche mentions only in passing the other major outcome of the aforementioned reconciliation, Old Greek Comedy, there can be little doubt that he holds it in similarly high esteem. In his "Attempt at a Self-Criticism," for example, he questions concerning "that madness out of which comic and tragic art developed—the Dionysian madness."[4] Are there perhaps neuroses of *health* (a question for psychiatrists)? Of the youth "and youthfulness of a people? . . . And regarding the origin of the tragic chorus: did those centuries when the Greek body flourished foamed over with health perhaps know ecstasies? Visions and hallucinations shared by entire communities or assemblies as a cult?"[5] Recalling the earlier discussion of divine madness, Nietzsche has recourse to Socrates's statement that madness may indeed bring the greatest blessings to a people, while the myth-destroying onset of reason, utilitarianism, and even democracy are symptoms of decline.

Although most of the plays performed at the Dionysian festivals have been lost, there are not only enough complete and near-complete works of Aeschylus, Sophocles, and Euripides to provide an excellent view of their unsurpassed quality but also enough in order for us to discriminate between them and to speculate sensibly on their development. This, precisely, is what Nietzsche has done in *The Birth of Tragedy*. However, the only extant whole comedies are those by Aristophanes, and while fragments of his contemporaries have survived there is insufficient evidence to discern similar developments.[6]

More significantly, it belonged to Nietzsche's great merit to have uncovered the underlying cheerfulness that animated both tragic poets and spectators. If this would be termed *pessimism*, it was a pessimism of strength and vigorous good health. Aristophanic comedy displayed boundless geniality, and so required no such account. Its celebration of life sounded in every phrase; there was no need to provide an interpretation of its underlying vital affirmation.

When the dynamic impulses that drive Greek tragedy wane, they are replaced by rational, that is, nonmythical substitutes that are smaller, weaker, and withdraw the spectator from vicarious participation in flourishing, robust life. Euripides embodies this decline, of which Nietzsche famously said: "Through him the everyday man forced his way from the spectators' seats onto the stage; the mirror through which formerly only grand and bold traits were represented now showed the painful fidelity that conscientiously produces even the botched outlines of nature.... The spectator now actually saw and heard his double on the Euripidean stage, and rejoiced that he could talk so well."[7]

The same decline occurs in comedy, to which anyone who has read the one surviving play of Menander can testify. *The Misanthrope* (*Duskolos*) consists of sober characters with wholly earthbound desires working their way through a plot so mild as to provoke that opposite kind of wonder, that is, how anything that dull by comparison could become so prominent and could serve as a model for the equally prosaic Roman comedies, which at least have the virtue of being satirical—albeit in a subtle and tame sense. Again, Nietzsche writes: "Civic mediocrity, on which Euripides built all his political hopes, was now given a voice, while heretofore the demigod in tragedy and the drunken satyr, or drunken demiman, in comedy, had determined the character of the language."[8]

Missing in such shrunken language is the very quality that constitutes its poetic nature, namely, *music*. Like Nietzsche's self-criticism, Greek poetry is sung—or perhaps more precisely, Greek poetry *sings*. The Homeric epics emblematize the apex of Apollonian art in which the beautifully individuated figures appear on the concealed subsoil of the Dionysian. Epic poetry, which finds its apotheosis in Archilochus, makes itself manifest—that is, it makes the world soul that sings through the inspired Archilochus, who is otherwise an ordinary man—in the folk song in which he curses the faithless Neobole.

Both strains reconcile in Greek tragedy. To speak prosodically, the Homeric dactylic hexameter fuses with the Dionysian dithyramb. To speak dramatically (as if these two can be separated in Greek tragedy), the sublime mythical figures in the epics merge with the howling and rending dismemberment of the world soul torn to pieces by the all-embracing Dionysian, and gave way to inferior progeny. However, like all that is beautiful and noble, Greek tragedy proved fragile and lost its heart and soul. The alteration of the position and role of the chorus signaled this decline: "[this alteration] . . . is the first step toward the *destruction* of the chorus, whose phases follow one another with alarming rapidity in Euripides, Agathon, and the New Comedy. Optimistic dialectic drives *music* out of tragedy . . . [the essence of which] can be interpreted only as a manifestation and projection into images of Dionysian states, as the visible symbolizing of music, as the dream-world of a Dionysian intoxication."[9]

Earlier in this text, Socratic dialectic serves as the enemy and annihilator of Greek tragedy, with Socrates and his ally Euripides erecting the standard of intelligibility and the appearance of verisimilitude, respectively. As will soon be demonstrated, Nietzsche's treatment of Socrates mirrors Schelling's conception of freedom and necessity. Just as in Schelling one finds the contradiction that animates all philosophical systems and all higher life, so in Socrates—in the image of Socrates— one finds the contradiction through which the history of Western life and thought can be comprehended. The Socrates who seeks to explicate all things in terms of intelligibility and so "cleanse" them of their dark, mythical content finds his guide in a *daimonion*. The *daimonion* is an anomalous kind of instinct—rather than driving one to act as instinct does in those who are healthy, in Socrates this instinct always *dissuades* from action. "While in all productive men it is instinct that is the creative affirmative force, and Consciousness acts critically and dissuasively, in Socrates it is instinct that becomes the critic and consciousness that becomes the creator—truly a monstrosity *per defectum!*"[10]

However, Nietzsche finds himself wrestling with another authentic Socrates, the Socrates who practices music on his final day. Using the Schellingian motif, the contradiction that is Socrates animates the entire history of Western philosophy. The "intelligible Socrates" may clash conceptually with the "music-practicing Socrates," but this contradiction on the strictly formal-logical level drives thought as this very contradiction is enacted.

Who is this "Socrates" that Nietzsche confronts? On one level, it is the Socrates we find inscribed in the accounts of Plato, Xenophon, Aristotle, and others who were either contemporaries or were close enough to his time to write about him. This element is no doubt alive in *The Birth of Tragedy*. However, in order to comprehend the Socratic role in the latter work, his essay titled "On the Uses and Disadvantages of History for Life" provides the needed insight.[11] There, one finds three modes of history delineated: (1) monumental history, which serves life by exhibiting great deeds of the past in order to show that great deeds in the future are possible; (2) antiquarian history, which serves life by demonstrating respect for past deeds and for their continuity through the present to the future, and (3) critical history, which serves life by smashing the idols of the past according to the new values that are to inform the future.

While it may seem that Nietzsche is "critical" with respect to the intelligible Socrates and "monumental" with respect to the music-practicing Socrates, in fact Socrates is a monument in both aspects. More precisely, the *historicized image* of Socrates constitutes the monument Nietzsche confronts, the monument that carries both aspects equally. The "intelligible Socrates" is an object of scorn and ridicule, rather than of negative appraisal. The "Music-Practicing Socrates," the one who was said to be composing hymns to Apollo and setting Aesop to music on his final day, provides passionate commendation rather than affirmative judgment: "Here we knock, deeply moved, at the gates of present and future: will this 'turning' lead to ever-new configurations of genius and of the *Socrates who practices music*? Will the net of art, whether it is called religion or science, that is spread over existence be woven even more tightly and delicately, or is it destined to be torn to shreds in the restless, barbarous, chaotic whirl that now calls itself 'the present?' "[12]

These questions hang in the air in *The Birth of Tragedy*, and they *yet* hang in the air suspended, hovering over all that we address. I suggest that we should not make too much of Nietzsche's changing view of Wagner. Wagner was clearly intended to iterate the structure of Nietzsche's Socratic reflections. In other words, Wagner functions as an *image* much in the manner that Socrates functions. However, the *pathos of distance* in the case of Wagner was absent; thus what should have functioned as a historical image became blurred with a living personage. In another less significant but still illustrative matter, consider Nietzsche's early proposal that Beethoven's "Ode to Joy" be imagined as a painting in order to depict the Dionysian.

It cannot be doubted, then, that the comments on Socrates occur for the sake of the present and the future, and not merely for matters of ancient scholarship. What, then, might we suggest about the status of these questions as they confront us here, in the United States, and now? The words "restless, barbarous whirl" have profound resonance for us. After a century that has seen genocides in Germany and Cambodia, world wars and regional wars without end, outbreaks of new and devastating diseases, not to mention the more lasting widespread poverty and political fecklessness, the call for a "tight and delicate" net of art drawn over existence sounds both vain and foolish, whether in retrospect or not.

The twentieth century has seen its share of prodigious artistic achievements in many if not all areas. A conclusive list of such achievements would be impossible to construct, but the following would appear on most: paintings by Cezanne and Picasso, poetry by Rilke and Eliot, fiction by Joyce and Beckett, music by Stravinsky and Charlie Parker, architecture by Mies van der Rohe and Frank Lloyd Wright, dance choreography by Diaghilev and Balanchine, film by Chaplin and Ozu. Just as likely, subterranean challenges to this list are possible. In any case, two conclusions can be reached from this exercise. First, these examples, and the very many that both extend and challenge the forms and/or contents that they exhibit, have contributed much insight, much pleasure, and much provocation to their spectators. Second, their influence has been undeniably fragmented even within the various genres, and more so among them.

The popular twentieth- and twenty-first century philosophical "movement" known as postmodernism (which is more of an internally disconnected series of more or less loosely affiliated styles) serves—or seems to serve—as the denial of the possibility of anything resembling "a tight and delicate net of art." If it can be said to affirm anything in that general area, it affirms a loose and coarse smorgasbord of "art-like" gestures. No doubt one can locate much talent and at least a kind of provocation in the work of, for example, Cindy Sherman and Damien Hirst. What one cannot locate so readily is the sense of interconnection, whether internal to the work or extending to a notion of community.

Somehow, retrospectives of Sherman's and Hirst's work are unlike retrospectives of the visual artists mentioned above, nor are they intended to resemble them—if indeed "resemblance" could be the appropriate word here. In any case, one cannot speak of the present state of art in terms of the classical age of Greek art, or in terms of the German classicism of Goethe and Schiller that was so familiar to Nietzsche even as he sought in vain a retrieve of unifying greatness in the operas of Wagner, or in terms of what we speak of—or once spoke of—as a modernism that heralded a new birth of freedom, a freedom that could take the form of rejection of traditional forms of authority, or their incorporation in newer, more creative ways.

What we can, however, and I say *must* acknowledge is the anterior ever-recurring inaccessibly accessible *prōtista Chaos genet'*, "first Chaos came into being," or in my rendering, "radically apart from all else has abyss come to presence," which allows anything discernible in any way to come forth at all. In this manner, Greek speaks English speaking Greek.

Notes

1. Friedrich Nietzsche, *The Birth of Tragedy*, in *The Birth of Tragedy and The Case of Wagner*, trans. Walter Kaufman (New York: Vintage Books, 1967), 24.
2. Ibid., 33.
3. Ibid., 24.
4. Ibid., 21.
5. Ibid.
6. See David Harvey and John Wilkins, eds., *The Rivals of Aristophanes* (London: Duckworth and the Classical Press of Wales, 2000).
7. Nietzsche, *Birth of Tragedy*, 77.
8. Ibid.
9. Ibid., 92.
10. Ibid., 88.
11. Nietzsche opens this essay by noting a "troubled feeling" he finds himself having as he contemplates the present condition of Germany and Europe. I explore this in my first publication, Bernard Freydberg, "Nietzsche's Socratic Task in 'Vom Nutzen und Nachteil der Historie für das Leben,'" in *Man and World*, ed. Robert Scharff, vol. 18 (Dordrecht: Martinus Nijhoff, 1985), 1985, 317–324.
12. Nietzsche, *Birth of Tragedy*, 98.

Bibliography

Aquinas, Thomas. *The Summa Theologica*. Translated by Anton C. Pegis. New York: Modern Library, 1948.
Aristotle. *The Basic Works of Aristotle*. Edited by Richard McKeon. Translated by W. D. Ross. New York: Random House, 1970.
Bacon, Francis and Montagu, Basil. *The Works of Francis Bacon*. Vol. 14. Philadelphia: Parry & McMillan, 1857.
Berkeley, George. *A Treatise Concerning the Principles of Human Knowledge* in *George Berkeley Collection: 5 Classic Works*. New York: Waxkeep, 2013.
Cunliffe, Richard John. *A Lexicon of the Homeric Dialect*. Norman: University of Oklahoma Press, 1963.
Deleuze, Gilles. *Empiricism and Subjectivity: An Essay on Hume's Theory of Human Nature*. New York: Columbia University Press, 2001.
———. "On Spinoza." *Lectures by Gilles Deleuze* (blog). February 2007. http://deleuzelectures.blogspot.com/2007/02/on-spinoza.html.
Descartes, Rene. *Discourse on Method and Meditations on First Philosophy*. Translated by Donald Cress. Indianapolis: Hackett, 1998.
Eliot, T. S. *The Waste Land*. Edited by Michael North. New York: W. W. Norton, 2000.
Empiricus, Sextus. *Against the Professors*. Translated by Robert Gregg Bury. Cambridge MA: Harvard University Press, 1949.
Euclid. *Elements*. Edited by Dana Densmore. Translated by Thomas L. Heath. Santa Fe: Green Lion Press, 2007.
Fichte, Johan Gottlieb. *Gesamtausgabe der Bayerischen Akademie der Wissenschaften*. Edited by Erich Fuchs, Reinhard Lauth, Hans Jacobs, and Hans Gliwitzky. Stuttgart-Bad Cannstatt: Frommann, 1964–2012.
———. *The Science of Knowledge*. Translated by Peter Heath and John Lachs. Cambridge: Cambridge University Press, 1982.
Freydberg, Bernard. *David Hume: Platonic Philosopher, Continental Ancestor*. Albany: State University of New York Press, 2012.
———. *Imagination in Kant's Critique of Practical Reason*. Bloomington: University of Indiana Press, 2005.
———. "Nietzsche's Socratic Task in Vom Nutzen und Nachteil der Historie für das Leben," in *Man and World, Vol. 18*. Edited by Robert Scharff. Dordrecht: Martinus Nijhoff Publishers, 1985.
———. *The Play of the Platonic Dialogues*. New York: Peter Lang, 1997.
———. "The Precise Kantian Origin of the Fichte-Schiller Conflict" in *7. Internationaler Kant-Kongresses, Akten II.2., Mainz 1990*. Bonn: Bouvier, 1991.

———. *Schelling's Dialogical Freedom Essay: Provocative Philosophy Then and Now*. Albany: State University of New York Press, 2008.
Grene, David and Lattimore, Richard. *The Complete Greek Tragedies, Vol. I-IV*. Chicago: The University of Chicago Press, 1991.
Harvey, David, and Wilkins, John. *The Rivals of Aristophanes*. London: Duckworth and the Classical Press of Wales, 2000.
Hegel, Georg Wilhelm Friedrich. *Aesthetics, Vol. I-II*. Translated by Thomas M. Knox. Oxford: Oxford University Press, 1975.
———. *Hegel's Science of Logic*. Translated by A. V. Miller. London: George Allen & Unwin Ltd., 1969.
———. *Logic, Erster Teil*. Berlin: Felix Meiner, 1971.
———. *Phenomenology of Spirit*. Translated by A. V. Miller. Oxford: Oxford University Press, 1977.
———. *Vorlesungen über der Geschichte der Philosophie, Band III*. Leipzig: Reklam, 1971.
Heidegger, Martin. *Being and Time*. Translated by Joan Stambaugh. Albany: State University of New York Press, 1996.
———. "Brief über den Humanismus" in *Wegmarken*. Frankfurt am Main: Vittorio Klostermann, 1967.
———. *Gesamtausgabe*. Frankfurt am Main: Vittorio Klostermann, 1975.
———. *An Introduction to Metaphysics*. Translated by Ralph Mannheim. Garden City: Doubleday Anchor, 1961.
———. *Letter on Humanism* in *Basic Writings*. Translated by David Farrell Krell. New York: Harper Collins, 1977.
———. *Martin Heidegger zum siebzigsten Geburtstag; Festschrift*. Pfullingen: G. Neske, 1959.
———. *Schellings Abhandlung Über das Wesen der menschlichen Freiheit (1809)*. Tübingen: Max Niemeyer Verlag, 1971.
———. *What is Called Thinking?* Translated by J. Glenn Gray. New York: Harper Torchbooks, 1972.
Heisenberg, Werner. *Der Teil und das Ganze*. Munich: R. Piper & Co. Verlag, 1969.
———. *Physics and Beyond: Encounters and Conversations*. New York: Harper Torchbooks, 1972.
Herder, Johann Gottfried. "Letters for the Advancement of Humanity" in *Another Philosophy of History and Selected Political Writings*. Translated by Ioannis Evrigenis and Daniel Pellerin. Indianapolis: Hackett, 2004.
Hesiod. *The Homeric Hymns and Homerica*. Translated by Hugh G. Evelyn-White. Cambridge: Harvard University Press, 1974.
———. *Theogony, Works and Days, Testimonia*. Translated by Glenn Most. Cambridge, MA: Harvard University Press, 2007.
Homer. *The Iliad of Homer*. Translated by Richard Lattimore. Chicago: The University of Chicago Press, 2011.

———. *The Odyssey of Homer*. Translated by Richard Lattimore. New York: Harper Perennial Modern Classics, 2007.
Hume, David. *An Inquiry Concerning Human Understanding*. Edited by Charles Hendel. Indianapolis: Bobbs-Merrill, 1977.
———. *A Treatise of Human Nature*. Edited by David F. Norton and Mary J. Norton. Oxford: Oxford Philosophical Texts, 2009.
Jammer, Max. *Einstein and Religion*. Princeton: Princeton University Press, 1999.
Kant, Immanuel. *Critique of Judgment*. Translated by J. H. Bernard. Indianapolis: Hafner, 1964.
———. *Critique of Practical Reason*. Translated by Lewis White Beck. Indianapolis: Bobbs-Merrill, 1956.
———. *Critique of Pure Reason*. Translated by Kemp Smith. New York: St. Martin's Press, 1965.
———. *Foundations of the Metaphysics of Morals*. Translated by Lewis White Beck. Indianapolis: Bobbs-Merrill, 1985.
———. *Religion within the Limits of Reason Alone*. Translated by Theodore M. Greene and Hoyt H. Hudson. New York: Harper and Brothers, 1960.
Kirk, G. S., Raven, J. E., and Schofield, M. *The Presocratic Philosophers*. Cambridge: Cambridge University Press, 1983.
Leibniz, Gottfried Wilhelm. *Discourse on Metaphysics and Other Essays*. Translated by Daniel Garber and Roger Ariew. Indianapolis: Hackett, 1991.
———. *The Monadology and Other Philosophical Writings*. Translated by Robert Latta. London: Oxford University Press, 1925.
Liddell, Henry, G. and Scott, Robert. *An Intermediate Greek–English Lexicon: Founded upon Liddell and Scott's Greek English Lexicon*. Oxford: Oxford University Press, 1975.
Locke, John. *An Essay Concerning Human Understanding*. Edited by Kenneth P. Winkler. Indianapolis: Hackett, 1996.
Menander. *Menander, Vol. I*. Translated by Geoffrey Arnott. Cambridge MA: Harvard University Press, 1979.
Nietzsche, Friedrich. *The Birth of Tragedy and The Case of Wagner*. Translated by Walter Kaufmann. New York: Vintage Books, 1967.
———. *Untimely Meditations*. Edited by Daniel Breazeale. Translated by Reginald L. Hollingdale. Cambridge: Cambridge University Press, 1997.
Ovid. *Metamorphoses*. Translated by Frank Justus Miller. Cambridge MA: Harvard University Press, 1984.
Parry, Milman. *The Making of Homeric Verse*. Oxford: Oxford University Press, 1971.
Plato. *Plato: Complete Works*. Edited John Cooper. Indianapolis: Hackett, 1997.
———. *The Republic of Plato*. Translated by Allan Bloom. New York: Basic Books, 1968.

Reichenbach, Hans. *The Rise of Scientific Philosophy*. Berkeley: University of California Press, 1968.
Sallis, John. *Being and Logos: Reading the Platonic Dialogues*. Bloomington: Indiana University Press, 1996.
———. *Chorology: On Beginnings in Plato's Timaeus*. Bloomington: Indiana University Press, 1999.
———. *Force of Imagination: The Sense of the Elemental*. Bloomington: Indiana University Press, 2000.
———. *On Translation*. Bloomington: Indiana University Press, 2002.
Schelling, Friedrich Wilhelm Joseph von. *First Outline of a System of the Philosophy of Nature*. Translated by Keith Peterson. Albany: State University of New York Press, 2004.
———. *Historical-Critical Introduction to the Philosophy of Mythology*. Translated by Mason Richey and Markus Zisselsberger. Albany: State University of New York Press, 2007.
———. *Ideen zu einer Philosophie der Natur als Einleitung in das Studium dieser Wissenschaft*, 1797 translated as *Ideas for a Philosophy of Nature: As Introduction to the Study of This Science*. Translated by Errol E. Harris and Peter Heath. Cambridge: Cambridge University Press, 1988.
———. *On University Studies*. Trans. Guterman (Athens: Ohio University Press, 1966).
———. *Philosophische Untersuchungen über das Wesen der menschlichen Freiheit und die damit zusammenhängenden Gegenstände* in *Friedrich Wilhelm Joseph von Schellings Sämmtliche Werke. VII Band, I Abteilung, 1805–1810*. Edited by K. F. A. Schelling. Stuttgart & Augsburg: J. G. Cotta, 1860.
———. *Philosophy of Art*. Translated by Douglas Stott. Minneapolis: University of Minnesota Press, 1989.
———. *Sämmtliche Werke*. Edited by K. F. A. Schelling. Stuttgart & Augsburg: J. G. Cotta, 1860.
———. *Schelling's Werke, nach der Originalausgabe in neuer Anordnung. Vol. I-VI*. Edited by Manfred Schröter. Munich: E. H. Beck, 1959.
———. *Schellings Werke, Vol. I. Jugendschriften 1793–1798*. Munich: C. H. Beck, 1965.
———. *Vorlesungun über die Methode des Akademischen Studiums* translated as *On University Studies*. Edited by Norbert Guterman. Translated by E. S. Morgan. Athens: Ohio University Press, 1966.
Schiller, Friedrich. *Über die ästhetische Erziehung des Menschen*. Stuttgart: Verlag Freies Geistesleben, 1989.
Schnackenberg, Gjertrud. *The Throne of Labdacus: A Poem*. New York: Farrar, Straus, and Giroux, 2000.
7. Internationaler Kant-Kongresses, Akten II.2., Mainz 1990. Bonn: Bouvier, 1991.

Sophocles. *Ajax* in *Sophocles Vol. I*. Translated by Hugh Lloyd-Jones. Cambridge MA: Harvard University Press, 1997.
Spinoza, Benedictus de. *Ethics* in *A Spinoza Reader: The Ethics and Other Works*. Edited and Translated by Edwin Curley. Princeton, NJ: Princeton University Press, 1994.
———. *The Letters*. Translated by Samuel Shirley. Indianapolis: Hackett, 1995.
———. *Principles of Cartesian Philosophy, with Metaphysical Thoughts*. Translated by Samuel Shirley. Indianapolis: Hackett, 1998.
———. *Theological-Political Treatise*. Edited by Jonathan Israel. Cambridge: Cambridge University Press, 2007.
Voltaire. *Candide*. Edited by Nicholas Cronk. New York: W. W. Norton Company Inc., 2016.

Index

Absolute Knowledge, 33
abstract ideas, 20
Achilles, 67
active/passive causality, 20–21
Adeimantus, 69
aesthetic philosophy, 11, 30, 83–85, 98, 101, 112
Aesthetics (Hegel), 83
Against the Grammarians (Sextus Empiricus), 112–13
Aias, 66–68
Aidos, 100
Alcibiades, 62–65
Alexander the Great, 115
Anagkē, 94
analytic geometry, 15
Analytic of the Sublime, 30
analytic philosophy, 16
Anaxagoras, 22, 52
Anaximander, 61
animal rationality, 95
Anselm of Canterbury, 56
anteriority, 33–37, 41–44, 72, 121
apeiron, 61
Aphrodite, 111
apodeixis, 8–9n7, 41
Apollinian/Dionysian duplicity, 7, 63, 68
Apollo, 72, 108
Apology (Plato), 42, 73
aporiai, 24
appearances, 32n24
a priori knowledge: and Kant's Pure Concepts of the Understanding, 24–27; and Leibniz's analytic philosophy, 17; and limits of modern philosophy, 2; and Schelling's *First Outline of a System of the Philosophy of Nature*, 90–91, 95; and Schelling's *Freiheitsschrift*, 115; and Schelling's transcendental idealism, 96–97

Aquinas, Thomas, 52, 56, 106
Ares, 100
Arges, 111
Aristotle: and atmosphere in Spinoza's thought, 60; and Cartesian mind/body dualism, 14; and causality, 106; and four causes, 53; and heterogeneity of modern philosophy, 11–12; and modern view of causality, 39–40; and necessity/causality relationship in Spinoza, 52; and Schelling's *Freiheitsschrift*, 110, 113–14
arithmetic, 17
art: and German Idealism, 83–84; philosophy of, 83–84; and Platonic inspiration, 4; and Schelling's *On University Studies*, 108; and Schelling's philosophy of art, 101–107; and Schelling's transcendental idealism, 97, 100
art drive, 93, 98–99
Ästhetische Briefe (Schiller), 85
atheism, 42
Athena, 66–68
atmosphere, 58, 62
Aufhebung (Hegel), 1
Augustine, 118–19

Bacon, Francis, 22–23
beauty, 4, 29, 64, 83
Beck, Lewis White, 26
becoming, 90–91
Being, 27, 107
Being and Logos: Reading the Platonic Dialogues (Sallis), 6
Being and Time (Heidegger), 48
Berkeley, George: and empiricism, 19–21; and freedom of the will, 45; and heterogeneity of modern philosophy, 11
bicentrality, 112, 114–19

The Birth of Tragedy, Or: Hellenism and Pessimism (Nietzsche), 31, 67–68
blind necessity, 93
Boreas and Oreithia myth, 8–9n7
Brontes, 111
bronze race of mankind, 100

calculus, 15
Candide (Voltaire), 17
Categories, 24–26, 91
causality: and Berkeley, 20–21; freedom/necessity interplay in Spinoza's rationalism, 45–47, 49; and Kant's aesthetic philosophy, 27–28; and Schelling's philosophy of art, 106; and Spinoza's necessity/causality relationship, 50–53
Cebes, 72–73
Chaos: and anteriority, 35–36; and manifestation of God, 116; and Schelling's *Freiheitsschrift*, 120, 121; and Schelling's *On University Studies*, 108; and Schelling's philosophy of art, 102
charity, 31
cheerfulness, 74, 78n82
chora, 6, 51, 113–14, 116
chorology, 51
Christianity: and contemporary view of inspiration, 5; and manifestation of God, 116–17; mythos of *agape*, 118; and Schelling's *On University Studies*, 109; and Schelling's philosophy of art, 105; and Spinoza's *Theological-Political Treatise*, 9n9
Chronos, 49, 99–100
cogito ergo sum, 45
cognition, 28–29
collectivism, 70
consciousness, 97, 98
Continental philosophy: and anteriority, 34; and freedom/necessity interplay in Spinoza's rationalism, 49; and heterogeneity of modern philosophy, 12–13; and logos/mythos dichotomy, 6; and political themes, 74. *See also specific philosophers*

contingency, 9n9, 23, 45
copula, 114–15
corporeal substance, 20
Critique of Judgment (Kant), 4, 29, 85
Critique of Practical Reason (Kant), 27–28, 46
Critique of Pure Reason (Kant), 24–25, 29, 89–90
Crito (Plato), 69
Cronus, 111
Cyclopes, 110–11

daimon/daimonion, 39–40, 64, 94, 98, 108, 127
darkness: and anteriority of God, 41; Apollinian/Dionysian duplicity, 7; as boundary of modern philosophy, 7; and final causality, 106; and freedom vs. necessity, 110; and genius concept, 98; and imagination in Spinoza's thought, 56; and impersonality of God, 75; and Kantian synthesis, 6, 24; and logos/mythos bridge, 5–6; and manifestation of God, 116–18; and nature of anteriority, 33; and necessity, 44; and objectivity of objects, 27; and reason/experience dichotomy, 11; and Schelling's bicentrality, 114–15; and Spinozist infinity, 62; suppression of Greek darkness in modern philosophy, 1
"Das Ich," 5, 86n8, 96
David Hume: Platonic Philosopher, Continental Ancestor, 21
death, 71–76
deduction, 16, 96
definition, 53
Deleuze, Gilles, 63–64
demigods, 100
Der Satz vom Grund (Heidegger), 34–35
Der Teil und das Ganze (Heisenberg), 58–59
Descartes, René: and anteriority, 34; and anteriority of God, 42; and freedom of the will, 45; and heterogeneity of modern philosophy, 11; and imagination in Spinoza's thought, 54–56; and Leibniz's analytic philosophy, 16–17;

and Locke's doctrinal opposition, 18; and mind/body dualism, 12–15; and Schelling's transcendental idealism, 100; and scope of modern philosophy, 1
desire, 29, 65
destiny, 98–99
determinism, 45, 59–60
Differenz des Fichteschen und Schellingschen Systems der Philosophie (Hegel), 82–83
Dionisius and Dionysian: Apollinian/Dionysian duplicity, 7, 62–63, 68; and divine madness, 37; and Nietzsche's "Attempt at a Self-Criticism," 123–24; and Nietzsche's *The Birth of Tragedy*, 125–27, 129; and Plato's view of Greek poetry, 3
Diotima, 62–63
Discourse on Metaphysics (Leibniz), 15–16, 115
Discourse on Method (Descartes), 13, 42, 54
divination, 4
divine imagination, 6–7
divine inspiration in Greek poetry, 2–3
divine knowledge, 115
divine logos, 58
divine madness, 3–4, 8n4, 8n7, 37, 121
divine nature, 44–45
doctrinal nature of modern philosophy, 2, 54
doctrine of ideas (Plato), 57
Doctrine of Science *(Wissenschaftslehre)*, 5
dualism, 100
dynamical sublime, 8n5

Earth, 35, 120
efficient cause, 53
eidos, 52
Einbilden, 102
Einstein, Albert, 59–60
Elements (Euclid), 41, 55, 75
Eliot, T. S., 20
emotions, 64–65
Empedocles, 113

empiricism: and Berkeley, 19–20; and heterogeneity of modern philosophy, 11; and Hume's Socratic heritage, 22; and intuition, 25–26; and Kantian synthesis, 24; Schelling's *First Outline of a System of the Philosophy of Nature*, 90–91; and Schelling's transcendental idealism, 97; and scope of modern philosophy, 1
episteme, 11
equality of men, 70
ergon (deed), 6
eros: and anteriority, 35, 36; and imagination in Spinoza's thought, 56; and "impersonality" of God, 75; and *Phaedrus*, 8–9n7, 8n4; and Plato's *Symposium*, 62–64; and Schelling's *Freiheitsschrift*, 120; and Spinoza's *Ethics*, 41
An Essay Concerning Human Understanding (Locke), 18
Esse est percipi, 19
eternality, 44
The Ethics (Spinoza): and atmosphere, 56–57, 60; context of, 40–42; and death, 71–72, 74–75; and *hoi polloi*, 69–70; and inspiration for philosophical inquiry, 4–5; necessity and causality in, 50; and Spinoza's *Symposium*, 65; and suppression of human imagination, 54–56
ēthos, 39
Euclid, 4, 27, 55–56, 57
Euclidean geometry, 27
eudaimonia, 39
Euripides, 2–3
evil. *See* good and evil
existence, 50, 107
experience, 23
extended substance *(res extensa)*, 13
external causes, 73

Fagles, Robert, 104
Fates, 49, 94, 98
fear of death, 71–76
Fichte, Johann Gottlieb: and contemporary view of inspiration, 4–5;

Fichte (cont.)
and "Das Ich," 86n8; and freedom/
necessity interplay in Spinoza's
rationalism, 46; and German Idealism,
82–85, 86n8; and inspiration for
philosophical inquiry, 5; and Kant's
Critique of Pure Reason, 89–90; and
Schelling's discourse, 6; and Schelling's
first published works, 87; and
Schelling's mythical philosophy, 88;
and Schelling's philosophy of nature,
92; and transcendental idealism,
95–96
final causes, 47, 53–54, 70–71, 75, 106
*First Outline of a System of the Philosophy
of Nature* (Schelling), 90–95
Force of Imagination (Sallis), 54
formal cause, 53
formal logic, 15, 110
Foundations of the Science of Knowledge
(Fichte), 86n8, 89–90
freedom: and art-drive, 98–99; and death
as anteriority, 72; freedom/necessity
interplay in Spinoza's rationalism,
44–50; and imagination in Spinoza's
thought, 54; and Kant's aesthetic
philosophy, 27–28; and necessity, 44–49,
95; and Schelling's *Freiheitsschrift,*
109–21, 118–21; and Schelling's
philosophy of nature, 93–94; and
Schelling's transcendental idealism, 98
freedom of thought, 9n9, 27
free will, 9n9, 42–43, 45–46
Freiheitsschrift (Schelling), 5, 82, 108,
109–21
French philosophy, 31

Gaia, 110–11
gender, 47
general ideas, 20
genius, 4, 97–98
geometry, 17, 93
German Idealism: and contemporary view
of inspiration, 4; and freedom/necessity
interplay in Spinoza's rationalism, 46;
and Hegel's rationalism, 81–86; and
Schelling's *Freiheitsschrift,* 113, 115; and
Schelling's philosophy of nature, 94; and
Schelling's transcendental idealism, 100
God: as anteriority, 41; and atmosphere in
Spinoza's thought, 60; and Cartesian
mind/body dualism, 14; and
empiricism, 19–21; and imperfections
of Nature, 70; impersonality of, 75; and
role of death, 72; and Schelling's
Freiheitsschrift, 116; and Schelling's *On
University Studies,* 109; and Spinoza's
definition of love, 65–68; and Spinozist
infinity, 61
good and evil dichotomy, 17–18, 46, 70, 73,
113, 118–20
Greek arts, 83–84, 96, 103–106
Greek mythos, 88–89, 94, 99–100
Greeks gods, 110–11
Grundlage der gesamten Wissenschaftslehre
(Fichte), 86n8, 89–90

Hades, 40, 73, 107, 108
happiness *(eudaimonia),* 29, 39
harmony, 105
hatred, 65–66
healing, 8n4
hearing, 58, 87–88, 101–102, 104
Heath, Peter, 86n8
Hecatonchieres, 110–11
Hegel, Georg Wilhelm Friedrich: and
anteriority, 33–34; and freedom/
necessity interplay in Spinoza's
rationalism, 46; and German Idealism,
81–84, 86; and inspiration for
philosophical inquiry, 5; as precursor
of Schelling, 7; and Schelling's
mythical philosophy, 88–89; and
Schelling's transcendental idealism,
99, 101; and scope of modern
philosophy, 1
Heidegger, Martin: and freedom/
necessity interplay in Spinoza's
rationalism, 48; and German Idealism,
82, 86; and Greek *ēthos,* 39; on Hegel's
rationalism, 81; on Parmenides and
Heraclitus, 43–44; and Schelling's
transcendental idealism, 99; and
Spinoza's intuition and infinitude, 61

Index

Heisenberg, Werner, 58–59
Hektor, 40
hen kai pan (one is all), 5
Heraclean (Magnet), 2–3
Heraclitus: and anteriority, 33, 42–44; and atmosphere in Spinoza's *Ethics*, 58–60; and freedom/necessity interplay in Spinoza's rationalism, 48–50; on role of *hoi polloi*, 68; and Schelling's *Freiheitsschrift*, 116; and Schelling's *On University Studies*, 108; and Schelling's philosophy of art, 103; and Schelling's philosophy of nature, 94; and Schelling's transcendental idealism, 99; and Spinoza's "intellectual love of God," 66; and Spinoza's intuition and infinitude, 61; and suppression of human imagination, 54
Herder, Johann Gottfried, 78n82
heroic race of mankind, 100
Hesiod, 35, 66, 75, 99–100, 108, 116, 120
history, 118–20
hoi polloi, 68–71
Homer, 2–3, 40, 47, 104, 106–107
honor, 64
hubris, 54
Hume, David: and Cartesian mind/body dualism, 15; and freedom/necessity interplay in Spinoza's rationalism, 45; and heterogeneity of modern philosophy, 11; and scope of modern philosophy, 2; Socratic heritage, 21–24
humility, 68, 70–71

Ideal City, 2–3
ideas and ideation: and atmosphere in Spinoza's thought, 57; and empiricism, 19–20; and freedom/necessity interplay in Spinoza's rationalism, 45; Locke's doctrinal opposition to Descartes, 18–19; and Plato's *Symposium*, 62–64; and role of death, 72, 75; Schelling's *First Outline of a System of the Philosophy of Nature*, 91; and Schelling's *On University Studies*, 108, 109; and Schelling's transcendental idealism, 101; and suppression of human imagination, 55
identity, law of, 115
ignorance, 23
The Iliad (Homer), 40, 104
imagination: and Cartesian mind/body dualism, 14–15; and forms of knowledge, 74–75; and Hegel's rationalism, 83; and Kantian synthesis, 8n5, 9n13, 24, 28, 91; and Kant's aesthetic philosophy, 25, 28–29; and Kant's practical philosophy, 8n5; and Schelling's philosophy of nature, 95; and Spinoza's God, 53–56
immortality of the soul, 72
Imperfectability, 93
imperfections of Nature, 70
impersonality of God, 75
independent causes, 53
indifference, 91–92, 102–103, 108, 116, 120, 125
induction, 23
infinitude, 44, 60–62
injustice, 74
An Inquiry Concerning Human Understanding (Hume), 15, 21
inspiration *(enthousiasmos)*, 2–4, 8n4, 108
intellect, 45, 75
intellectual love of God, 65
An Introduction to Metaphysics (Heidegger), 43–44
intuition, 25–26, 42–43, 55–56, 91; and Kantian synthesis, 26
Ion (Plato), 2
iron race of mankind, 100

Judeo-Christianity, 117
judgment, 29, 89–90

Kant, Immanuel: aesthetic philosophy of, 24–31; on appearances, 32n24; and contemporary view of inspiration, 4–5; and "Das Ich," 86n8; and freedom/necessity interplay in Spinoza's rationalism, 45–47; and heterogeneity of modern philosophy, 11; and

Kant, Immanuel (cont.)
inspiration for philosophical inquiry, 5; and role of imagination, 8n5; and Schelling's discourse, 6; and Schelling's early works, 89–90; and Schelling's *Freiheitsschrift*, 111–14; and Schelling's *On University Studies*, 108; and Schelling's philosophy of nature, 91; and scope of modern philosophy, 1; on the sublime, 8n5; and transcendental idealism, 95–98
Klang (sonority), 102

Lachesis, 40, 49
Lachs, John, 86n8
language, 20
Lattimore, Richard, 104–105
Laut (sound), 102
Laws (Plato), 57
Lectures concerning the Method of Academic Studies (Schelling), 101, 107–109
Leibniz, Gottfried: and freedom/necessity interplay in Spinoza's rationalism, 45; and heterogeneity of modern philosophy, 11, 12; influence on analytic philosophy, 15–18; and Schelling's *Freiheitsschrift*, 115; and Schelling's philosophy of art, 106; and scope of modern philosophy, 2
Letter on Humanism (Heidegger), 39
Locke, John, 11, 18–19, 45, 51
logic, 30, 34
logos: and anteriority of God, 43; freedom/necessity interplay in Spinoza's rationalism, 50; and Kant's aesthetic philosophy, 26, 28; and Schelling's *Freiheitsschrift*, 110, 115–16; Schelling's Spinoza critique, 40; and Spinoza's *Ethics*, 43; and Spinoza's intuition and infinitude, 61
love (*eros*), 5, 65–68

Magnet, 2–3
magnetism, 102–103
The Making of Homeric Verse (Parry), 104
material cause, 53

materialism, 21
mathematical sublime, 8n5
mathematics, 13, 19
Matter (corporeal substance), 20
mechanical laws, 13–14
medical diagnosis, 13–14
melancholy, 74
melody, 8n4, 47, 104–106
memory, 54, 75
Mendelsohn, Moses, 24
metaphysical philosophy: forms of, 32n17; and Hume's Socratic heritage, 21; and Kantian synthesis, 24; and Kant's aesthetic philosophy, 31; and Leibniz, 16; and Schelling's philosophy of nature, 91
mind (*nous*), 3
mind/body dualism, 12–15
Monadology (Leibniz), 17, 115
monism, 43
monotheism, 117
morality, 28–29, 60, 78n83, 108
moral philosophy, 21
moral purpose, 29–30
Moses, 9n9
Muses, 3, 8n4, 35–36, 75
music, 103–106
mythical language, 6
mythical philosophy, 87
Myth of Er, 6, 40, 94, 107
mythos: Apollinian/Dionysian duplicity, 7; and Presocratic thinkers, 43–44; and Schelling's discourse, 7; and Schelling's *Freiheitsschrift*, 110; and Schelling's mythical philosophy, 88; and Schelling's philosophy of nature, 94; and Spinoza's *Ethics*, 40

nature: and anteriority of God, 37, 41; and Berkeley's notion of causality, 20–21; and inspiration for philosophical inquiry, 5; natural law, 59; natural philosophy, 21, 90–91; natural sciences, 22, 30–31, 34; and role of *hoi polloi*, 70; and Schelling's *Freiheitsschrift*, 111, 116–20
necessity: freedom/necessity interplay in Spinoza's rationalism, 44–50; and

necessity/causality relationship in Spinoza, 50–53; and Schelling's *Freiheitsschrift*, 110; and Schelling's philosophy of art, 107; and Schelling's philosophy of nature, 93–94
negative metaphysics, 32n17
Nemesis, 100
Newton, Isaac, 12
Nichomachean Ethics (Aristotle), 39
Nietzsche, Friedrich, 4, 7, 67–68, 117
nonrational thought, 1
noumenon, 24, 27
Nous (Anaxagoras), 22, 52

objectivity, 27, 59
observation, 23
Odysseus, 66–67
Odyssey (Homer), 104
Oedipus the King (Sophocles), 47–48
On the Freedom of the Will (Augustine), 118–19
ontology, 51–52
On University Studies (Schelling), 107–109
opinion, 55, 74–75
oral philosophy, 87–88
oral poetry, 103–104
otherness, 33, 36, 102
Ouranos, 110–11

paganism, 109, 116–17
pain, 29
Pandora, 88–89
panta rhei, 104
pantheism, 116, 117–18
Paralogisms of Pure Reason, 30, 114
Parmenides: and anteriority of God, 42–44; and freedom/necessity interplay in Spinoza's rationalism, 48–49, 48–50; and imagination in Spinoza's thought, 54; on role of *hoi polloi*, 68–69; and Schelling's philosophy of art, 103, 107; and Schelling's philosophy of nature, 94; and Spinoza's intuition and infinitude, 61
Parry, Milman, 104
Parthenogenesis, 111
perception, 19–20, 22

perfection, 63–64
Peterson, Keith R., 92
Phaedo (Plato), 22, 52, 71, 72
Phaedrus (Plato), 3, 4, 8–9n7, 36, 41, 57
phenomenology, 21
Phenomenology of Spirit (Hegel), 33, 81
phenomenon, 27
Philebus (Plato), 57
Philosophy of Art (Schelling), 89, 101–107
philosophy of nature, 82, 90
Physics (Aristotle), 52
Piraeus, 40
pistis (Platonic trust), 4
Plato: and anteriority, 36; and *apodeixis*, 8–9n7; and atmosphere in Spinoza's thought, 56–60; and Hume's Socratic heritage, 21–23; and logos/mythos bridge, 6; and necessity/causality relationship in Spinoza, 51; Platonic dialogues, 69–71; Platonic inspiration, 3–4; Platonic solids, 58–59; Platonic trust *(pistis)*, 4; and Schelling's *Freiheitsschrift*, 110, 112–13; and Schelling's mythical philosophy, 88–89; and Schelling's *On University Studies*, 108; and Schelling's philosophy of art, 103, 107; and Schelling's transcendental idealism, 98; and Spinoza's *Ethics*, 40, 62–68; and Spinoza's "intellectual love of God," 66
pleasure, 29, 57
poetry, 2–3, 8n4, 47
polytheism, 42, 117
positive metaphysics, 32n17
Postulates of Empirical Thought, 27
potentiality, 119
power, 119
practical philosophy, 27, 46
"The Precise Kantian Origin of the Fichte-Schiller Conflict" (Freydberg), 84–85
prediction, 107
preestablished harmony doctrine, 17
primary qualities, 19, 20
Principles *(Grundsätze)*, 25
Principles of Cartesian Philosophy (Spinoza), 54

Principles of Human Knowledge
(Berkeley), 20
Principles of the Pure Understanding
(Kant), 25, 27, 91
probability, 15
Problem of Induction, 23
Prometheus, 88–89
prophesy, 8n4
Pure Concepts of the Understanding,
6, 24
pure intuition, 25–26
purposivness, 29–30
Pythagoras, 112–13

quantum theory, 59

races of man, 99–100
rationalism: Hegel, 81; and heterogeneity
of modern philosophy, 11; and Kantian
synthesis, 24; and Leibniz, 15–18; and
logos/mythos bridge, 6; and Schelling's
philosophy of nature, 95; and
Schelling's transcendental idealism,
101; and scope of modern philosophy, 1;
and Spinoza's influence on modern
philosophy, 75
rational language, 6
"The Real Side of the Form of Art"
(Schelling), 101–102
reason: and anteriority, 34–35;
Apollinian/Dionysian duplicity, 7; and
atmosphere in Spinoza's thought, 58;
and Cartesian mind/body dualism,
14–15; and freedom/necessity interplay
in Spinoza's rationalism, 49–50; and
German Idealism, 83; and Hegel's
rationalism, 81; and imagination in
Spinoza's thought, 54–55; and
inspiration for philosophical inquiry, 5;
and Kant's aesthetic philosophy, 30;
and Locke's *reflection*, 19; and
Schelling's *Freiheitsschrift*, 115; and
scope of modern philosophy, 1, 2; and
Spinoza's *Ethics*, 41; and Spinoza's
influence on modern philosophy, 75;
and standard narrative of modern
philosophy, 11

reflective judgment, 30
Reichenbach, Hans, 56–58
religion: and art, 128; and contemporary
view of inspiration, 4–5; and human
freedom, 119; and inspiration for
philosophical inquiry, 5; and
monotheism, 117; and necessity/
causality relationship in Spinoza, 52;
and paganism, 117–18; and role of death,
74–75; and Spinoza's *Theological-
Political Treatise*, 9n9
Religion within the Limits of Reason Alone
(Kant), 5, 119
repentance, 68, 70–71
Republic (Plato), 6, 40, 69, 71, 107
Republic of Geniuses, 64
res cogitans/res extensa, 45, 100
rhythm, 103–106
The Rise of Scientific Philosophy
(Reichenbach), 56–57
ruling images, 50

sacred art, 101
Sallis, John: and logos/mythos dichotomy,
6; and necessity/causality relationship
in Spinoza, 51, 52; and Schelling's
Freiheitsschrift, 113–14; on Spinoza's
Ethics, 40–41; and suppression of
human imagination, 54
Schall (resonance), 102
Schelling, Friedrich Wilhelm Joseph: on
anteriority, 33; and anteriority of God,
41; and contemporary view of
inspiration, 4–5; and divine
imagination, 6–7; *First Outline of a
System of the Philosophy of Nature*,
90–95; and freedom/necessity interplay
in Spinoza's rationalism, 46;
Freiheitsschrift, 109–21; and German
Idealism, 82–86; Hegel as precursor, 7;
and logos/mythos bridge, 5–7; on
mythical philosophy, 87–89; and
necessity/causality relationship in
Spinoza, 50; *Philosophy of Art*, 101–107;
System of Transcendental Idealism,
95–101; *On University Studies*, 107–109;
Vom Ich als Prinzip der Philosophie

oder Über das Unbedingte im menschlichen Wissen, 89–90
Schelling's Dialogical Freedom Essay (Freydberg), 115–16
Schemata, 25–26, 91
Schiller, Friedrich, 84–85
Schnackenberg, Gjertrud, 47
Scholasticism, 14, 32n17, 52
Schopenhauer, Arthur, 64
science, 12, 22, 23, 90–91, 112
Science of Logic (Hegel), 81
sculpture, 83
secondary qualities, 19, 20
self-caused beings, 50
self-knowledge, 8–9n7, 13, 30
self-unity, 30
sensation, 18–19
Sense Certainty, 33
serial intuition, 60–61
Seven Years' War, 17
Sextus Empiricus, 112–14
Shakespeare, William, 105–106
Simmias, 72–73
Simplicius, 49, 61
skeptical philosophy, 23
Snellius, 17
Socrates: and anteriority, 36–37; and *apodeixis*, 41; and Apollinian/Dionysian duplicity, 68; and Aristotle's four causes, 53; and God of Spinoza's *Ethics*, 42; and Hume's Socratic heritage, 21–23; and inspiration for philosophical inquiry, 11; intellectualization of ethics, 57; and the judgment of *hoi polloi*, 69–71; and the myth of *Eros*, 8–9n7; and necessity/causality relationship in Spinoza, 52; and perspective on death, 71–74; and Plato's *Symposium*, 64–65; and Schelling's *On University Studies*, 108; Socratic ignorance, 60; Socratic philosophical method, 21–22
Sophist (Plato), 103
Sophocles, 66, 105
Spindle of Necessity, 107
Spinoza, Baruch: and anteriority, 33–34; and atmosphere, 56–60; and contemporary view of inspiration, 4; and divine imagination, 6–7; equation of God with nature, 5; and eros in Plato's *Symposium*, 62–68; excommunication of, 74; and German Idealism, 81–82; and God as anteriority, 41–44; and Greek *ēthos*, 39–41; and heterogeneity of modern philosophy, 11; and imagination, 53–56; and inspiration for philosophical inquiry, 5; and intuition and infinitude, 60–62; and the judgment of *hoi polloi*, 68–71; and limits of modern philosophy, 1–2; and nature of death, 71–76; and necessity/causality relationship, 50–53; and necessity in philosophy, 44–50; and Schelling's discourse, 6–7; and Schelling's *Freiheitsschrift*, 116, 120; and Schelling's philosophy of art, 106; and Schelling's transcendental idealism, 96
spirits, 20–21, 33
spontaneous intuition, 26
Steropes, 111
striving, 92
subjectivity, 19, 59, 83
sublimity, 4, 8n5, 30
substance, 15–17, 19, 33–34, 50
sufficient reason (*Der Satz vom Grund*), 34–35, 106, 115
supernatural, 45
suprarational intuition, 55–56
Symposium (Plato), 57, 62–68
synthesis, 6, 8n5, 9n13, 24, 26, 28
System of Transcendental Idealism (Schelling), 95–101

tabula rasa, 18
telos, 11–12
tertiary qualities, 19
Thales, 22
Theaetetus (Plato), 11
Theogony (Hesiod), 35, 75, 110
A Theological-Political Treatise (Spinoza), 5, 9n9
Theophrastus, 61
theoretical philosophy, 46

thinking substance *(res cogitans)*, 13–14
Third Antinomy (Kant), 27, 111
thought, 62, 81
three Moirai (Fates), 49
The Throne of Labdacus (Schnackenberg), 47–48
Timaeus (Plato), 6, 51, 58, 92, 114, 116
Titans, 110–11
Transcendental Aesthetic, 26
Transcendental Deductions, 24
transcendental idealism, 95–101
Treatise of Human Nature (Hume), 22
Trojan War, 67

"Über Geist und Buchstab in der Philosophie" (Fichte), 85
unconsciousness, 81, 97
understanding, 4, 28–29
unity of Greek thought, 107
unity/separation duplicity, 97

values, 60
virtue, 40
Voltaire, 17
Vom Ich als Prinzip der Philosophie oder Über das Unbedingte im menschlichen Wissen (Schelling), 89–90

Western metaphysics, 31
Wissenschaftslehre (Fichte), 5, 84
wonder, 11
Works and Days (Hesiod), 99–100
written philosophy, 87–88

Zeus, 100

BERNARD FREYDBERG is Scholar in Residence at Duquesne University. He is author of *Imagination in Kant's Critique of Practical Reason* (Indiana University Press) and *Philosophy and Comedy: Aristophanes, Logos, and Eros* (Indiana University Press), as well as six other books, including *The Thought of John Sallis: Phenomenology, Plato, Imagination*.

Lightning Source UK Ltd.
Milton Keynes UK
UKOW01f0019170817
307469UK00001B/2/P